外国人学汉语100句系列

英语版

eriencing Chinese

Cultural Communication in China

体验汉语® **100** 句

文化类

顾 问 曾晓渝

编 者 孙 易 孙 雪

谷 峰

译 者 刘小梅

高等教育出版社

Higher Education Press

总 策 划　　刘　援

编　　者　　孙　易　孙　雪　谷　峰

译　　者　　刘小梅

英语审订　　Erin Harper

策划编辑　　徐群森

责任编辑　　金飞飞　鞠　慧

封面设计　　彩奇风

版式设计　　高　瓦

插图选配　　陆　玲　杨晓静

责任校对　　金飞飞　鞠　慧

责任绘图　　九月天空

责任印制　　宋克学

尊敬的读者：

　　您好！

　　欢迎您选用《体验汉语100句》系列丛书。

　　随着经济全球化的不断发展和中国国力的增强，世界范围内学习汉语的人数不断增加。为满足不同国度、不同领域、不同层次汉语学习者的需求，我社策划、研发了《体验汉语100句》系列丛书。该系列丛书包含生活类、留学类、商务类、旅游类、文化类、体育类、公务类、惯用表达类等诸方面，有针对性地帮助汉语学习者快捷地掌握相关领域中最常见、最实用的中文表达。

　　为满足各国汉语学习者的实际需要，每册书还配有英语、日语、韩语、法语、德语、俄语、西班牙语、泰语、印尼语等九个语言版本，今后还将开发更多语种的版本。

　　愿本书成为您步入汉语世界的向导，成为您了解中国的桥梁，也希望您提出意见和建议。欢迎您随时与我们联系。

高等教育出版社

2007年1月

前言

本书是《体验汉语100句》系列中的文化类。

《体验汉语100句》系列覆盖生活、留学、商务、旅游、文化、体育、公务、惯用表达等诸多方面，有针对性地帮助汉语学习者掌握相关领域中最常见、最实用的汉语表达。

本书精选了反映中国文化的100个常用句，归入17个项目。学习者在学习基础汉语的同时，可了解中国文化，掌握相关的专门用语和习惯表达方式。

特 点

1. 按功能项目归类。
2. 核心句型尽量使用问句，具有很强的实践性。
3. 一问一答的口语编排形式，互动性强。
4. 所有中文句子都标有拼音和英语译文。
5. 附录收入了十二属相、中国的节日和中国历史年代简表。

结 构

本书中每句话的学习都包括常用句、对话、DIY和注释四个部分。

• 常用句

全书共收录100个常用句，每个句子都用汉字、拼音和英语译文清楚地标明了句子的写法、拼音和意义。

• 对话

对话内容均为在真实场景下使用的常用句，以帮助学习者理解句子，学会使用和应答。

• DIY

帮助学习者灵活应用每个常用句，提供替换练习。

• 注 释

用英语介绍、解释中国文化现象，便于学习者理解、记忆。

中华文明，源远流长；中国文化，生动博大。衷心希望您通过本书，不仅能提高口语能力，还能了解中国文化，在体验中国文化的同时，也体验学习的快乐。

编 者

Foreword

The *Experiencing Chinese 100* series contains phrases pertaining to living, studying, traveling, sports, cultural communication, business communication, official communication, popular Chinese idioms and many more areas of interest. This book is *Experiencing Chinese 100 (Cultural Communication in China)*.

This book is specifically aimed to help the Chinese learners understand the most practical and often used communications. We have chosen 100 practical Chinese sentences and divided them into 17 different categories. This book will not only help those who are interested in Chinese culture enhance their basic language competence, it will also help them have a good understanding of Chinese culture and master phrases and expressions in specific situations.

Features

1. For convenience, the book can be referred to according to category of function.

2. For pragmatic purposes, the frequently used sentences are usually in the interrogative forms.

3. For interaction, the book is arranged in the form of dialogues.

4. All of the sentences are written in Chinese and *Pinyin* with English translations and annotations.

5. The appendix includes 12 Chinese Years of Animals, Chinese Holidays and A Brief Chinese Chronology.

Structure

This book includes: Frequently Used Sentences (FUS), Conversation, DIY and Notes.

FUS: There are a total of 100 sentences, each written in both Chinese characters and *Pinyin*, accompanied by an English translation and clear grammar explanations.

Conversation: Places FUS in a realistic setting, thus allowing readers to better understand the sentence's meaning, usage, as well as appropriate responses.

DIY: After each sentence, DIY provides several exercises allowing readers to practice appropriate usage.

Notes: The Chinese cultural phenomena are explained in English for the better understanding and memorization of international friends.

Chinese civilization dates back to thousands of years ago and it still enjoys its vivid and profound cultural heritage. We sincerely hope that this book will not only improve the oral Chinese of our readers, at the same time, it will help you have a good understanding and experience of Chinese culture and bring you the joy of learning.

Author

目录 Contents

您是赵一平先生吧？
Nín shì Zhào Yīpíng xiānsheng ba?

Are you Mr. Zhao Yiping?

● 您是赵一平先生吧？
Nín shì Zhào Yīpíng xiānsheng ba?

● 对，我是赵一平。
Duì, wǒ shì Zhào Yīpíng.

● Are you Mr. Zhao Yiping?
● Yes, I am.

您是＿＿＿＿＿＿吧?
nín shì   ba

李华同学
Lǐ Huá tóngxué

classmate Li Hua

王芳小姐
Wáng Fāng xiǎojiě

Miss Wang Fang

张平教授
Zhāng Píng jiàoshōu

Professor Zhang Ping

NOTES

Xiānsheng (Mr.) is a honorific title given to an adult man. In Chinese, the surname and name are always put before the title, for instance, "Zhāng xiānsheng (Mr. Zhang)", "Wáng xiǎojiě (Miss Wang)", and so on.

"赵"是您的姓，"一平"是您的名字，是吧？

"Zhāo" shì nín de xìng, "Yīpíng" shì nín de míngzi, shì ba?

Is "Zhao" your surname and "Yiping" your given name?

- "赵" 是您的姓，"一平" 是
  "Zhāo"　 shì nín de xìng，　 "Yīpíng"　 shì

  您的名字，是吧？
  nín de　 míngzi,　 shì　 ba?

- 太对了。
  Tài duì le.

- Is "Zhao" your surname and "Yiping" your given name?
- Yes, you are right.

_____是您的姓，_____是您
　　shì nín de xìng　　　　shì nín
的名字，是吧？
de míngzi　 shì ba

李林
Lǐ Lín

Li Lin

张爱华
Zhāng Àihuá

Zhang Aihua

金大成
Jīn Dàchéng

Jin Dacheng

NOTES

　　In Chinese, there are only surnames and
given names, no middle names. Unlike English
names, Chinese names begin with the surname and
end with the given name. Each person's name is
endowed with a certain meaning, especially with his/
her parents' hope or best wishes.

孔子姓"孔",名字叫"子"吗?
Kǒngzǐ xìng "Kǒng", míngzi jiào "Zǐ" ma?

Is Kongzi's surname Kong and given name Zi?

● 孔子姓"孔",名字叫"子"吗?
Kǒngzǐ xìng "Kǒng", míngzi jiào "Zǐ" ma?

● 错了!孔子的名字是"丘",
Cuò le! Kǒngzǐ de míngzi shì "Qiū",

"子"是别人对他的尊称。
"Zǐ" shì biérén duì tā de zūnchēng.

○ Is Kongzi's surname Kong and given name Zi?
● No! Kongzi's given name is Qiu, and Zi is a honorific title given to him.

_____姓____，名字叫____吗？
xìng　　　míngzi jiào　　ma

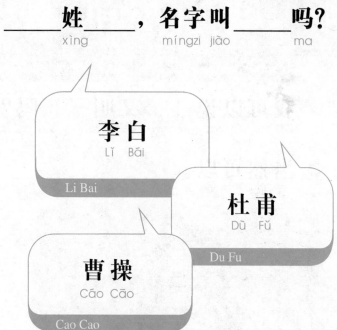

李 白
Lǐ　Bái

Li Bai

杜 甫
Dù　Fǔ

Du Fu

曹 操
Cáo　Cāo

Cao Cao

NOTES

Kongzi (Confucius) (551 – 479BC) was a great philosophical thinker and educator in ancient China. He established a philosophical school called "Confucianism". The ideology of "benevolence" put forward by him has greatly influenced Chinese culture and Chinese people's way of thinking. His thought has spread to many Asian countries such as Japan, the Republic of Korea and DPR Korea. As a result, Confucius is regarded as a symbol of Chinese culture, or even a symbol of Oriental culture.

7

我可以说孔子又叫孔丘吗？
Wǒ kěyǐ shuō Kǒngzǐ yòu jiào Kǒng Qiū ma?

May I say that Kongzi also goes by the name of Kong Qiu?

○ 我可以说孔子又叫孔丘吗？
  Wǒ kěyǐ shuō Kǒngzǐ yòu jiào Kǒng Qiū ma?

● 当然可以。
  Dāngrán kěyǐ.

○ May I say that Kongzi also goes by the name of Kong Qiu?

● Yes, indeed.

我可以说＿＿＿＿又叫＿＿＿＿吗?
wǒ kěyǐ shuō yòu jiào ma

蛐蛐儿
qūqur

cr
cricket

蟋蟀
xīshuài

cricket

重阳节
Chóngyángjié

Double Ninth Festival

登高节
Dēnggāojié

Double Ninth Festival

NOTES

Ancient Chinese used "bó (eldest brother)", "zhòng (second brother)", "shū (third brother)" and "jì (youngest brother)" to show the sequence of the brothers. For example, the historical figure Sun Quan also goes by the name Sun Zhongmou, in which Zhong indicates that he is the second son of the family. If a family has only three sons, ancient Chinese also use "mèng", "zhòng" and "jì" to show the sequence of the brothers.

9

她 是 我 姑 姑。

Tā shì wǒ gūgu.

She is my aunt (from the paternal side).

● 照片上这个女的是谁？

Zhàopiàn shang zhège nǚ de shì shuí?

● 她是我姑姑。

Tā shì wǒ gūgu.

○ Who's the woman in the picture?

● She is my aunt (from the paternal side).

她是我＿＿＿＿＿。
tā shì wǒ

奶奶
nǎinai

grandmother
(from the paternal side)

姥姥
lǎolao

grandmother
(from the maternal side)

舅妈
jiūmā

aunt
(wife of the mother's brother)

NOTES

　　"Wǒ gūgu (my aunt)" can also be expressed as "wǒ de gūgu (my aunt)". In Chinese, "de" is an auxiliary word indicating subordination or possession. It is a common practice to omit "de" between the pronoun and the noun showing kindred. For instance, we can say "wǒ bàba (my father)" as well as "wǒ de bàba (my father)", yet the usage of "wǒ shūbāo (my bag)" is restricted. In the most cases we say " wǒ de shūbāo (my bag)". The reason for this difference exists in the way of Chinese thinking. Chinese people regard the relationship between their kindred and themselves as much closer than that between someone and his/her body parts or possessions. For this reason, it is not a usual practice to insert words between the pronoun and the noun showing kindred.

11

6

姑姑是不是也可以叫姨妈？
Gūgu shìbushì yě kěyǐ jiào yímā?

Can "gūgu" also be addressed as "yímā"?

- 姑姑是不是也可以叫姨妈？
  Gūgu shìbushì yě kěyǐ jiào yímā?

- 不行。姑姑是爸爸的姐妹，
  Bù xíng. Gūgu shì bàba de jiěmèi,

  姨妈是妈妈的姐妹。
  yímā shì māma de jiěmèi.

- Can "gūgu" also be addressed as "yímā"?
- No, "gūgu" refers to the father's sister, and "yímā" refers to the mother's sister.

12

_____是不是也可以叫_____?
shìbushì yě kěyǐ jiào

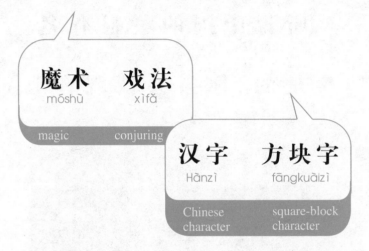

魔术　戏法
móshù　xìfǎ

magic　　conjuring

汉字　方块字
Hànzì　fāngkuàizì

Chinese character　square-block character

The ways of addressing relatives reflect the kinship among Chinese people. In general, people of Han nationality classify relatives into two branches, that is, relatives from the paternal side and relatives from the maternal side. Read the table below:

your father's	father	mother	brothers	sisters
you call him/her	yéye	nǎinai	bófù/shūshu	gūgu
your mother's	father	mother	brothers	sisters
you call him/her	lǎoye	lǎolao	jiùjiu	yímā

7

听说中国的茶很有名。

Tīngshuō Zhōngguó de chá hěn yǒumíng.

I hear that Chinese Tea is well-known.

● 听说中国的茶很有名。
Tīngshuō Zhōngguó de chá hěn yǒumíng.

● 是的，你尝尝铁观音吧。
Shìde, nǐ chángchang Tiěguānyīn ba.

● I hear that Chinese Tea is well-known.

● Yes, indeed. Please have a taste of Tieguanyin.

14

听说中国的 ＿＿＿＿＿ 很有名。
tīngshuō Zhōngguó de   hěn yǒumíng

长城
Chángchéng

the Great Wall

黄山
Huángshān

Huangshan Mountain

瓷器
cíqì

chinaware

NOTES

Tieguanyin, one variety of Chinese tea, is produced in Anxi County, Fujian Province. It is a type of oolong tea. Black tea, green tea and oolong tea are the three major categories of Chinese Tea.

小姐，我要一个麻婆豆腐。
Xiǎojiě, wǒ yào yí gè Mápó Dòufu.

Hi, miss, I'd like to order fried bean curd with chilli sauce.

○ **小姐，我要一个麻婆豆腐。**
Xiǎojiě, wǒ yào yí gè Mápó Dòufu.

● **好的，请稍等。**
Hǎode, qǐng shāo děng.

○ Hi, miss, I'd like to order fried bean curd with chilli sauce.
● O.K., just a moment, please.

我要一个_____。
wǒ yào yí ge

酸辣汤
Suānlàtāng

sour and spicy soup

水煮鱼
Shuǐzhǔyú

boiled fish

宫保鸡丁
Gōngbǎo Jīdīng

fried diced chicken with peanuts

NOTES

"Fried bean curd with chilli sauce" is a special dish in Sichuan cuisine. It is spicy and can be ordered in almost every restaurant. There are eight schools of Chinese cuisine, which are Shandong, Sichuan, Guangdong, Fujian, Jiangsu, Zhejiang, Hunan and Anhui cuisine.

四川菜和广东菜比起来怎么样？

Sìchuāncài hé Guǎngdōngcài bǐ qǐlái zěnmeyàng?

How does Sichuan cuisine compare to Guangdong cuisine?

● **四川菜和广东菜比起来**
Sìchuāncài hé Guǎngdōngcài bǐ qǐlái

怎么样？
zěnmeyàng?

● **四川菜有点儿辣，广东菜**
Sìchuāncài yǒudiǎnr là, Guǎngdōngcài

比较清淡。
bǐjiào qīngdàn.

● How does Sichuan cuisine compare to Guangdong cuisine?
● Sichuan cuisine is a bit spicy, and Guangdong cuisine is light in flavor.

_____和_____比起来
　　　　hé　　　　　bǐ　qǐlái

怎么样？
zěnmeyàng

中国菜　意大利菜
Zhōngguócài　　　Yìdàlìcài

Chinese cuisine　Italian cuisine

鱼香肉丝　古老肉
Yúxiāng　Ròusī　　Gǔlǎoròu

fish-flavored shredded　fried pork slices with
pork in hot sauce　　　sweet and sour sauce

NOTES

　　　　Sichuan cuisine refers to a group of dishes developed in Sichuan Province. It can be further classified into two branches, Chengdu cuisine and Chongqing cuisine. Guangdong cuisine mainly refers to the dishes developed in Guangdong Province. It can also be classified into three branches, which are Guangzhou, Chaozhou and Dongjiang cuisine.

我听说中国人很喜欢在吃饭的时候喝茶。
Wǒ tīngshuō Zhōngguórén hěn xǐhuan zài chīfàn de shíhou hē chá.

I hear that Chinese people like to drink tea when having meals.

● 我听说中国人很喜欢在吃饭
Wǒ tīngshuō Zhōngguórén hěn xǐhuan zài chīfàn

的时候喝茶。
de shíhou hē chá.

● 是啊，茶还可以在饭前或者
Shì a, chá hái kěyǐ zài fàn qián huòzhě

饭后喝。
fàn hòu hē.

● I hear that Chinese people like to drink tea when having meals.

● Yes, they do. They also have tea before or after meals.

我听说＿＿＿＿＿＿＿＿。
wǒ tīngshuō

中国的自行车很多
Zhōngguó de zìxíngchē hěn duō

There are many bicycles in China.

中国茶特别好喝
Zhōngguó chá tèbié hǎo hē

Chinese tea is especially tasty.

在中国买东西比较便宜
zài Zhōngguó mǎi dōngxi bǐjiào piányi

Commodities are cheap in China.

NOTE

The practice of drinking tea has a long history in China. Originally, tea was used as a herbal medicine for detoxification. Tea was first grown in the Qin and Han Dynasties. Later, in the Tang Dynasty, a man named Lu Yu summarized the practice and history of preparing and drinking tea in a work entitled *Book of Tea*, and he created a totally new way of preparing tea. From then on, tea became widespread in China.

中国南方和北方的饮食习惯一样吗?

Zhōngguó nánfāng hé běifāng de yǐnshí xíguàn yíyàng ma?

Do southerners have the same dietary customs as northerners?

- **中国南方和北方的饮食**
  Zhōngguó nánfāng hé běifāng de yǐnshí

  习惯一样吗?
  xíguàn yíyàng ma?

- **南方人喜欢吃清淡的,北方人**
  Nánfāngrén xǐhuan chī qīngdàn de, běifāngrén

  喜欢吃味儿重点儿的。
  xǐhuan chī wèir zhòng diǎnr de.

- Do southerners have the same dietary customs as northerners?
- Southerners like light-flavored food, while northerners have a more heavy taste.

22

中国南方和北方的
Zhōngguó nánfāng hé běifāng de

＿＿＿＿＿一样吗？
yíyàng ma

气候
qìhòu

climate

方言
fāngyán

dialect

消费水平
xiāofèi shuǐpíng

consumption level

NOTES

On the whole, Chinese people, whether from the south or from the north, pay great attention to their diets. They demand that food should embody beautiful colors, fragrant smells and good tastes. However, they have great differences in their tastes. There is a saying that, "South sweet, north salty, east spicy, west sour." This means that southerners like sweet food, while northerners are fond of salty food; people from the eastern part of the country like spicy food, while people from the western part of country are fond of sour food.

新 年 好 ！
Xīnnián hǎo !

Happy New Year!

● 新 年 好 ！
Xīnnián hǎo !

● 新 年 好 ！
Xīnnián hǎo !

● Happy New Year!
● Happy New Year!

_____!

生 日 快 乐
shēngrì   kuàilè

Happy Birthday!

一 路 顺 风
yílù   shùnfēng

Bon Voyage!

身 体 健 康
shēntǐ   jiànkāng

Keep fit!

NOTES

In China, at the very beginning of the Chinese Lunar Year, that is, the 1st day of the 1st lunar month, there comes the most important festival of the year — the Spring Festival. The day before the Spring Festival is called Lunar New Year's Eve. During the Spring Festival, a number of entertainments and activities are very popular, such as setting off firecrackers and pasting Spring Festival couplets, to name a few. Family members get together to have their Lunar New Year dinner, and dumpling or New Year's cake is a popular delicacy. Watching the Spring Festival Gala has become a new custom as well. It is said that the custom of setting off firecrackers originated for the purpose of driving away a monster called "nian", and pasting Spring Festival couplets intends to ward off evil spirits.

我们贴完春联以后干什么?
Wǒmen tiē wán chūnlián yǐhòu gàn shénme?

What shall we do after we finish pasting Spring Festival couplets?

● 我们贴完春联以后干什么?
Wǒmen tiē wán chūnlián yǐhòu gàn shénme?

● 我们再去放鞭炮。
Wǒmen zài qù fàng biānpào.

● What shall we do after we finish pasting Spring Festival couplets?

● Let's go and set off firecrackers.

我们_____以后干什么？
wǒmen   yǐhòu gàn shénme

逛完故宫
guàng wán Gùgōng

visited the Forbidden City

吃完饭
chī wán fàn

finished the meal

买完东西
mǎi wán dōngxi

finished shopping

NOTES

The custom of writing and pasting Spring Festival couplets was derived from the practice of hanging a peach talisman on the door. A full Spring Festival couplet consists of the first couplet, the second couplet, and a streamer.

27

端午节是怎么起源的？
Duānwǔjié shì zěnme qǐyuán de?

How did the Dragon Boat Festival come into being?

● 端午节是怎么起源的？
    Duānwǔjié shì zěnme qǐyuán de?

● 端午节是为了纪念著名
    Duānwǔjié shì wèile jìniàn zhùmíng

诗人屈原。
shīrén Qū Yuán.

● How did the Dragon Boat Festival come into being?
● The Dragon Boat Festival was set up in memory of the famous poet Qu Yuan.

_____是怎么起源的？

shì zěnme qǐyuán de

圣诞节
Shèngdànjié

Christmas

元宵节
Yuánxiāojié

Lantern Festival

情人节
Qíngrénjié

Valentine's Day

NOTES

The Dragon Boat Festival falls on the 5th day of the 5th lunar month. It was set up in memory of the famous patriotic poet Qu Yuan (circa 340–278BC). On the Dragon Boat Festival, dragon boat competitions are often held, and families everywhere eat zongzi (glutinous rice wrapped up in reed leaves). Small kids often wear colorful threads around their necks, wrists and ankles. It is said that the colorful threads have the power to ward off evil spirits.

端午节跟春节吃的东西不一样吧？
Duānwǔjié gēn Chūnjié chī de dōngxi bù yíyàng ba?

We eat different food during the Dragon Boat Festival than during the Spring Festival, don't we?

● 端午节跟春节吃的东西不
　Duānwǔjié gēn Chūnjié chī de dōngxi bù

　一样吧？
　yíyàng ba?

● 对。端午节吃的是粽子，
　Duì. Duānwǔjié chī de shì zòngzi,

　春节吃的是饺子。
　Chūnjié chī de shì jiǎozi.

● We eat different food during the Dragon Boat Festival than during the Spring Festival, don't we?

● Yes. During the Dragon Boat Festival, we eat zongzi (glutinous rice wrapped up in reed leaves), and during the Spring Festival, we have jiaozi (dumplings).

_____跟_____不一样吧？
gēn　　　　bù yíyàng ba

春节　元旦
Chūnjié　Yuándàn

Spring Festival　New Year's Day

中国的龙　西方的龙
Zhōngguó de lóng　xīfāng de lóng

Chinese Dragon　Western Dragon

NOTES

　　Zongzi is a special food for the Dragon Boat Festival. Zongzi is made of glutinous sticky rice stuffed in reed leaves and boiled in water. In the north, zongzi tastes sweet. Ingredients such as beans, dates or finely grated coconut will be added to the stuffing in zongzi. In the south, however, zongzi can be salty in flavor, and meat can be used as the stuffing.

中国有没有情人节?
Zhōngguó yǒu méiyǒu Qíngrénjié?

Is there a Valentine's Day or not in China?

● **中国有没有情人节?**
Zhōngguó yǒu méiyǒu Qíngrénjié?

● **七夕可以看作是中国的**
Qīxī kěyǐ kànzuò shì Zhōngguó de

情人节。
Qíngrénjié.

● Is there a Valentine's Day or not in China?
● Double Seventh Festival can be regarded as the Chinese Valentine's Day.

中国有没有_____?
Zhōngguó yǒu méiyǒu

母亲节
Mǔqīnjié

Mother's Day

儿童节
Értóngjié

Children's Day

泼水节
Pōshuǐjié

Water-Splashing Day

NOTES

Almost everyone in China, young and old, is very familiar with the story behind the Double Seventh Festival. A long time ago, there was a poor cowherd, Niulang. He fell in love with Zhinü, "the Girl Weaver". Unfortunately, the King and Queen of Heaven were furious finding out that their granddaughter had gone to the world of Man and taken a husband. Thus, the couple was separated by the Milky Way and can only meet once a year on the 7th day of the 7th lunar month. The Double Seventh Festival is not a public holiday in China. However, it is still a day to celebrate the annual meeting of the loving couple. Not surprisingly, many people consider the Double Seventh Festival the Chinese Valentine's Day.

33

17

过元宵节要吃什么？
Guò Yuánxiāojié yào chī shénme?

What is the special food for the Lantern Festival?

● **过端午节要吃粽子，那么，**
Guò Duānwǔjié yào chī zòngzi, nàme,

过元宵节要吃什么？
guò Yuánxiāojié yào chī shénme?

● **过元宵节人们要吃元宵。**
Guò Yuánxiāojié rénmen yào chī yuánxiāo.

● So if zongzi is the special food for the Dragon Boat Festival, what is the special food for the Lantern Festival?
● People eat yuanxiao (a kind of sweet dumpling made of glutinous rice flour) to celebrate the Lantern Festival.

过_____要吃什么？
guò　　　　　　yào chī shénme

生日
shēngrì

birthday

中秋
zhōngqiū

Mid-Autumn Festival

冬至
dōngzhì

winter solstice

NOTES

"Yuanxiao", dumplings made of glutinous rice flour, first appeared in the Song Dynasty. They are essentially stuffed glutinous rice flour balls. When boiled, they sink and then surface in the water, so they are also termed as "floating balls (fuyuanzi)". Because they look like a full moon, these dumplings are called "tangyuan" as well.

我应该送什么礼物？
Wǒ yīnggāi sòng shénme lǐwù?

What present should I give?

● 明天是林华的生日，
Míngtiān shì Lín Huá de shēngrì,

我应该送什么礼物？
wǒ yīnggāi sòng shénme lǐwù?

● 我还没想好，不过你千万
Wǒ hái méi xiǎng hǎo, búguò nǐ qiānwàn

别送闹钟。
bié sòng nàozhōng.

● Tomorrow is Lin Hua's birthday. What present should I give him?

● I haven't decided yet, but you definitely should not give him a clock.

我应该送什么_____?
wǒ yīnggāi sòng shénme

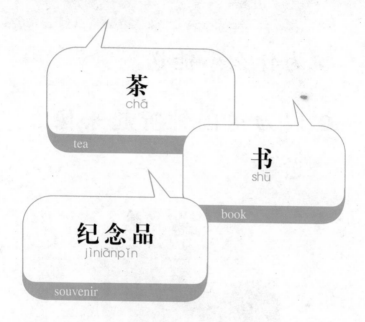

茶
chá

tea

书
shū

book

纪念品
jìniànpǐn

souvenir

NOTES

When giving presents, people from the Republic of Korea often choose very pragmatic things such as a tube of toothpaste or a bar of soap. Chinese people, however, tend to choose tea, wine, handiworks or local specialties. If you go to a wedding ceremony, a set of exquisite tablewares is a good choice.

为什么不能送闹钟?
Wèishénme bù néng sòng nàozhōng?

Why can't we give clocks as presents?

● **为什么不能送闹钟?**
Wèishénme bù néng sòng nàozhōng?

● **因为送闹钟听起来像**
Yīnwèi sòng nàozhōng tīng qǐlái xiàng

送终。
sòngzhōng.

● Why can't we give clocks as presents?
● It's because the pronunciation of "giving a clock" (sòngzhōng) sounds very much like "paying last respects" in Chinese.

为什么不能送＿＿＿？
wèishénme　bū néng sòng

梨
lí

pear

伞
sǎn

umbrella

菊花
júhuā

chrysanthemum

Chinese people tend to avoid giving clocks as presents because the pronunciation of clock (zhōng) in Chinese sounds like the pronunciation of "ending", and "sōngzhōng" conveys images of death and funerals. In Chinese, when people talk about "death", they use expressions such as "bú zài le (not existing), zǒu le (gone away), guòshì le (passed away)". In Shanghai dialect, the pronunciation of "beginning" (shǐ) sounds very much like "book" (shū), so if Shanghai people do give a clock as a present, they will at the same time present a book as well, as this means to wish a person a good beginning as well as a good ending.

"正"不是应该读 zhèng 吗?
"Zhēng" bū shì yīnggāi dú zhèng ma?

Shouldn't "正" be pronounced "zhèng"?

● "正"不是应该读 zhèng 吗?
"Zhēng" bū shì yīnggāi dú zhèng ma?

中国人怎么都说"正月"呢?
Zhōngguórén zěnme dōu shuō "zhēngyuè" ne?

● 因为秦始皇叫嬴政,所以
Yīnwèi Qínshǐhuáng jiào Yíng Zhèng, suǒyǐ

古人得避开他的名讳。
gǔrén děi bìkāi tā de mínghuì.

正月初一

● Shouldn't "正" be pronounced "zhèng"? Why do Chinese people pronounce "正月" as "zhēngyuè?"

● This is because the name of the first emperor of China was "Ying Zheng", so ancient people thought the pronunciation was taboo.

_____不是_____吗？
　　 bú shì　　　　 ma

你　　回家了
nǐ　　huíjiā　le

you　　　go home

明天　　　　放假
míngtiān　　　fàngjià

tomorrow　　take a holiday

The Chinese feudal society lasted for 2,000 years, in which the emperor enjoyed the highest power. In this society, there were kept strict hierarchies which were reflected in the way people used language. There were taboos on certain subjects. For instance, there are words one should avoid saying directly, such as the names of the emperor, the king's family and one's ancestors.

41

我一不小心把你的杯子打碎了。

Wǒ yí bù xiǎoxīn bǎ nǐ de bēizi dǎsuì le.

I accidentally broke your cup.

● 哎呀！真对不起，我一不小心
　Āiya! Zhēn duìbuqǐ, wǒ yí bù xiǎoxīn

　把你的杯子打碎了。
　bǎ nǐ de bēizi dǎsuì le.

● 没关系。"岁岁平安"嘛。
　Méiguānxi. "Suìsuì píng'ān" ma.

● Oh! I'm so sorry. I accidentally broke your cup.
● No worries. "A safe and sound year will follow."

42

我一不小心把你的＿＿＿＿了。
wǒ yí bù xiǎoxīn bǎ nǐ de　　　le

铅笔弄丢
qiānbǐ nòngdiū

lose your pencil

名字写错
míngzi xiěcuò

spell your name wrongly

车撞倒
chē zhuàngdǎo

knock down your bicycle

NOTES

Chinese people have strong taboos about breaking things during the New Year's Festival. People believe that it is ominous to drop a bowl, dish, or cup on the ground and cause it to break into pieces. To offset the possible misfortune, people often comment in the moment: "suìsuì píng'ān (a safe and sound year)", because the pronunciation of year 岁 (suì) in Chinese is the same with that of smash 碎 (suì).

22

这些名字多难听啊！
Zhèxiē míngzi duō nántīng a!

These names sound terrible!

● 有些孩子叫 "狗剩"、"栓子"、
Yǒuxiē háizi jiào "Gǒushèng", "Shuānzi",

"二蛋" 什么的，这些名字多
"Èrdàn" shénme de, zhèxiē míngzi duō

难听啊！
nántīng a!

● 这你就不懂了，因为大人希望
Zhè nǐ jiù bù dǒng le, yīnwèi dàrén xīwàng

他们平平安安，健健康康。
tāmen píngpíng'ān'ān, jiànjiànkāngkāng.

○ Some kids are named "Gousheng", "Shuanzi", and "Erdan". These names sound terrible!

● You don't understand. It is because their parents wish them good health and hope that they grow up smoothly.

这些____多____啊！
zhèxiē   duō   a

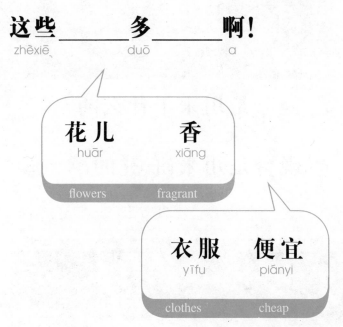

花儿　香
huār   xiāng

flowers   fragrant

衣服　便宜
yīfu   piānyi

clothes   cheap

NOTES

Traditionally, people believe that a name is a part of one's life, so it cannot be called casually. If a child's name is called by a demon, his spirit will be trapped and carried away by the demon. So, parents often give their children vulgar names for the purpose of protecting them. According to tradition, there are two kinds of names that a demon will not say: one is the names of Buddhist monks and Taoist priests, which a demon does not dare to say; the other is poor names, which a demon does not like to say.

23

砚台是用来干什么的?

Yàntai shì yònglái gàn shénme de?

What do people use inkslabs for?

● **砚台是用来干什么的?**
Yàntai shì yònglái gàn shénme de?

● **砚台是用来研墨的。**
Yàntai shì yònglái yánmò de.

● What do people use inkslabs for?
● Inkslabs are used for rubbing inksticks.

_____是用来干什么的？
shì yònglái gàn shénme de

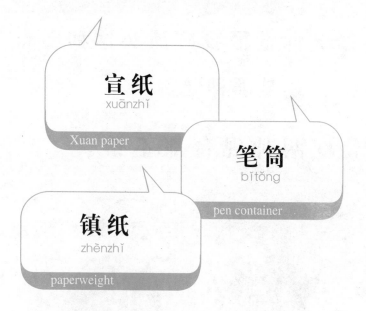

宣纸
xuānzhǐ

Xuan paper

笔筒
bǐtǒng

pen container

镇纸
zhēnzhǐ

paperweight

NOTES

The Chinese writing brush, inkstick, paper and inkslab are termed "the four treasures of the study", for they are indispensable tools for ancient Chinese intellectuals who were good at writing and painting. Necessary articles in a study also included pen containers, penholders and paperweights.

24

你觉得我应该买这种砚台还是那种砚台?
Nǐ juéde wǒ yīnggāi mǎi zhè zhǒng yàntai háishì nà zhǒng yàntai?

Which inkslab do you think I should buy, this one or that one?

● 你 觉 得 我 应 该 买 这 种 砚台
Nǐ juéde wǒ yīnggāi mǎi zhè zhǒng yàntai

还 是 那 种 砚台?
háishì nà zhǒng yàntai?

● 两 种 砚 台 都 不 错。
Liǎng zhǒng yàntai dōu búcuò.

● Which inkslab do you think I should buy, this one or that one?

● Both are pretty good.

你觉得我应该买这种＿＿＿＿
nǐ juéde wǒ yīnggāi mǎi zhè zhǒng

还是那种＿＿＿＿?
háishì nǎ zhǒng

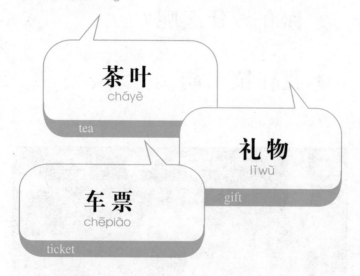

茶叶
cháyè
tea

礼物
lǐwù
gift

车票
chēpiào
ticket

NOTES

The inkslab first came into being in the early years of the Shang Dynasty. It gradually took its form along with the use of the inkstick. Inkslabs are made of stone, pottery, brick or jade. Among them, the most famous are the ones produced in Guangdong and Anhui Provinces. The inkslabs produced in Duanxi of Gaoyao, Guangdong Province bear the name "Duanyan", and the ones produced in Shexian County, Anhui Province have the name "Sheyan".

25

你在做什么呢？

Nǐ zài zuō shénme ne?

What are you doing?

● 你在做什么呢？
  Nǐ zài zuō shénme ne?

● 我在拉二胡。
  Wǒ zài lā èrhú.

● What are you doing?
● I'm playing erhu.

你在____什么呢？
nǐ zài   shénme ne

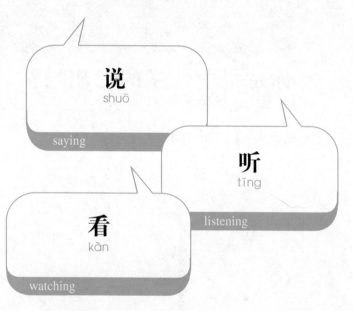

说
shuō
saying

听
tīng
listening

看
kān
watching

NOTES

There are four kinds of Chinese musical instruments: string instrument, wind instrument, percussion instrument, and tanbo instrument. Erhu is one of the most famous string instruments. Besides it, there are still other string instruments, such as jinghu, banhu and matouqin. Flute, sheng and suona are members of wind instrument; drum, gong, muyu, bangzi and cymbals are very common instruments of percussion instrument; and yu-kin, liuqin, guzheng and yangqin belong to tanbo instrument.

26

你是跟老师学的二胡吗？

Nǐ shì gēn lǎoshī xué de èrhú ma?

Do you study erhu with a teacher?

● **你是跟老师学的二胡吗？**
Nǐ shì gēn lǎoshī xué de èrhú ma?

● **我是自学的。**
Wǒ shì zìxué de.

○ Do you study erhu with a teacher?

● No, I study by myself.

52

你是＿＿＿＿＿学的二胡吗？
nǐ shì   xué de   ěrhú   ma

跟朋友
gēn péngyou

with friends

在中国
zài Zhōngguó

in China

NOTES

　　Erhu, also known as the "Chinese violin", is a fascinating string instrument with unique charm. It is good for performing music that conveys emotions of deep sorrow, and it can also depict magnificent atmosphere. Famous erhu players include Hua Yanjun (A Bing) and Liu Tianhua. Famous musical pieces played on the erhu include Èrquán Yìngyuè (*The Moon Reflected on the Second Spring*) and Jiānghéshuǐ (*Riven of Sorrow*). Now erhu is an important solo instrument as well as an essential instrument in the orchestra.

27

这是在布上画的还是在纸上画的？

Zhè shì zài bù shang huà de háishì zài zhǐ shang huà de?

Is the picture painted on canvas or on paper?

● 这是在布上画的还是在
Zhè shì zài bù shang huà de háishì zài

纸上画的？
zhǐ shang huà de?

● 这是在宣纸上画的。
Zhè shì zài xuānzhǐ shang huà de.

○ Is the picture painted on canvas or on paper?

● It is painted on Xuan paper.

这是_____还是_____?
zhè shì   hǎishì

真的　假的
zhēn de   jiǎ de

genuine   fake

琵琶　月琴
pípá   yuèqín

Pipa   Yukin

NOTES

Chinese paintings are done with water and ink, so they are called as "water and ink paintings", and are also known as "traditional Chinese paintings". When painting pictures, artists intentionally leave blank space for the purpose of arousing people's imagination. This is especially true when painting landscapes. With figure paintings, Chinese artists do not pay so much attention to human dissection and the scale among different objects, but rather emphasize the charm of their work.

28

这幅画儿的作者是齐白石吗？

Zhè fú huàr de zuòzhě shì Qí Báishí ma?

Is Qi Baishi the painter of this painting?

● 这幅画儿的作者是齐白石吗？
Zhè fú huàr de zuòzhě shì Qí Báishí ma?

● 对极了！齐白石老人最喜欢
Duì jí le! Qí Báishí lǎorén zuì xǐhuan

画虾了。
huà xiā le.

○ Is Qi Baishi the painter of this painting?
● Yes, exactly. Master Qi was fond of painting shrimps.

这幅画儿的作者是 _____ 吗?
zhè fú huàr de zuòzhě shì _____ ma

张大千
Zhāng Dàqiān

Zhang Daqian

徐悲鸿
Xú Bēihóng

Xu Beihong

达·芬奇
Dá Fēnqí

Leonardo da Vinci

NOTES

Qi Baishi (1864–1957) is one of the most renowned painters of traditional Chinese painting. He is best-known for his paintings of shrimps. Another very famous painter is Xu Beihong, who enjoys great fame for his paintings of horses.

29

新娘子为什么要穿红色的衣服?
Xīnniángzi wēishénme yào chuān hóngsè de yīfu?

Why should a bride wear a red gown at her wedding?

● 新娘子为什么要穿红色
Xīnniángzi wēishénme yào chuān hóngsè

的衣服?
de yīfu?

● 因为中国人认为红色是
Yīnwèi Zhōngguórén rènwéi hóngsè shì

吉祥的颜色。
jíxiáng de yǎnsè.

● Why should a bride wear a red gown at her wedding?
● Because Chinese people believe red is a lucky color.

＿＿＿为什么要穿＿＿＿的衣服？
wèishénme yào chuān　　de　yīfu

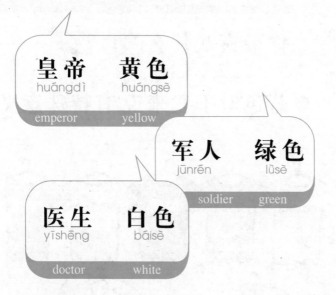

皇帝　黄色
huángdì　huángsè

emperor　yellow

军人　绿色
jūnrén　lǜsè

soldier　green

医生　白色
yīshēng　báisè

doctor　white

NOTES

From ancient times, Chinese people began to use the color red. The imperial family believed that the color red was a symbol of their prestige, wealth, confidence, power and inviolability. In architecture, red has long been used in decoration, and is believed to resemble wealth and good luck.

59

30

你最喜欢什么颜色？
Nǐ zuì xǐhuan shénme yánsè?

What's your favorite color?

● 你最喜欢什么颜色？
Nǐ zuì xǐhuan shénme yánsè?

● 蓝色对于我来说 有特殊意义。
Lánsè duìyú wǒ lái shuō yǒu tèshū yìyì.

YELLOW GREEN BLUE WHITE RED

○ What's your favorite color?
● Blue has a special meaning for me.

你最喜欢什么＿＿＿？
nǐ zuì xǐhuan shénme

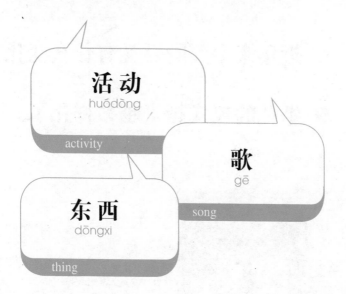

活动
huódòng

activity

歌
gē

song

东西
dōngxi

thing

NOTES

In ancient China, there were strict rules on the use of colors. Emperor Yang in the Sui Dynasty (Suíyángdì) prohibited ordinary people to wear yellow. From then on, the color yellow became a special color only for emperors to use. In traditional Chinese culture, on happy occasions such as weddings, red is often used, and colors such as black or blue are avoided. At funerals, people usually dress in white or black.

31

近年来中国的婚礼有什么变化?
Jìnniánlái Zhōngguó de hūnlǐ yǒu shénme biànhuà?

Are there any changes concerning wedding customs in China?

- **近年来中国的婚礼有什么变化?**
  Jìnniánlái Zhōngguó de hūnlǐ yǒu shénme biànhuà?

- **婚礼的仪式越来越多样化了。**
  Hūnlǐ de yíshì yuèláiyuè duōyànghuà le.

幸福

美满

I feel safe with you.
I want to say that
I love you very much and always will.

- Are there any changes concerning wedding customs in China in recent years?
- Wedding ceremonies are becoming increasingly diversified.

近年来_____有什么变化?
jìnniánlái　　　　　yǒu shénme biànhuà

中国
Zhōngguó

China

中美关系
ZhōngMěi guānxì

Sino-American relationship

气候
qìhòu

climate

NOTES

Nowadays, when it comes to the wedding ceremony, young people have a variety of choices. Holding banquets is the most popular option, while some choose to hold parties or go travel. Still, there are people who prefer to join collective wedding ceremonies held by certain organizations.

32

你打算在哪里办喜事？
Nǐ dǎsuàn zài nǎlǐ bān xǐshì?

Where do you think your wedding ceremony will be held?

● **你打算在哪里办喜事？**
Nǐ dǎsuàn zài nǎlǐ bān xǐshì?

● **这件事要由我女朋友家决定。**
Zhè jiàn shì yào yóu wǒ nǚpéngyou jiā juédìng.

○ Where do you think your wedding ceremony will be held?

○ Well, it's up to my girlfriend's family to decide.

你打算在哪里_____?
nǐ dǎsuàn zài nǎlǐ

结婚
jiéhūn

hold a wedding ceremony

吃午饭
chī wǔfàn

have lunch

学汉语
xué Hànyǔ

learn Chinese

NOTES

China is a country with many nationalities, and each nationality has different wedding ceremony traditions. For instance, the Han nationality wedding ceremony traditionally decided a marriage by the words of the parents and the matchmakers. An engagement was considered proper only if it was matched by a go-between and betrothal gifts were given to the bride's family. Marriages usually took place between families of the same social status. Nowadays, people enjoy freedom of love and marriage, and the wedding ceremony has been greatly simplified.

33

祝你们百年好合！

Zhù nǐmen bǎinián hǎohé!

An ever-happy marriage to you!

● 祝你们百年好合！
Zhù nǐmen bǎinián hǎohé!

● 谢谢！
Xièxie!

○ An ever-happy marriage to you!
● Thank you very much!

祝你们＿＿＿＿＿！
zhū nǐmen

早生贵子
zǎoshēng guìzǐ

May you have children soon!

白头偕老
báitóu xiélǎo

May you remain happily married to a ripe old age!

万事如意
wànshì rúyì

Best wishes to you!

NOTES

When you go to the wedding ceremony of a Chinese couple, you are expected to say some words of good wishes. For example, you can say "báitóu xiélǎo(may you remain happily married to a ripe old age), bǎinián hǎohé(an ever-happy marriage to you)", or "zǎoshēng guìzǐ (may you have children soon)".

34

参加中国人的婚礼要特别注意什么吗?

Cānjiā Zhōngguórén de hūnlǐ yào tèbié zhùyì shénme ma?

Is there anything special that I should pay attention to when I go to a Chinese wedding?

● 参加中国人的婚礼要特别
Cānjiā Zhōngguórén de hūnlǐ yào tèbié

注意什么吗?
zhùyì shénme ma?

● 当然。除了要说祝福的话
Dāngrán. Chúle yào shuō zhùfú de huà

以外，还要送贺礼。
yǐwài, hái yào sòng hèlǐ.

○ Is there anything special that I should pay attention to when I go to a Chinese wedding?

● Yes, indeed. Besides expressing good wishes with words, you should bring a gift to express your congratulations.

_____要特别注意什么吗？

yào tèbié zhùyì shénme ma

参加中国人的葬礼

cānjiā Zhōngguórén de zànglǐ

go to a Chinese funeral

去西藏旅行

qù Xīzàng lǚxíng

go traveling in Tibet

学习汉语

xuéxí Hànyǔ

learn Chinese

NOTES

When you go to the wedding of a Chinese couple, you are expected to say some words of good wishes as well as give them a gift. The general practice is to give a sum of money enclosed in a red envelope. The sum of money you give is decided by the intimacy of your relationship with the couple.

这是我做的菜，请您尝尝吧。
Zhè shì wǒ zuò de cài, qǐng nín chángchang ba.

I cooked this dish myself. Please have a taste.

● 这 是 我 做 的 菜 ， 请 您
Zhè shì wǒ zuò de cài, qǐng nín

尝 尝 吧 。
chángchang ba.

● 真 是 色 香 味 俱 全 啊 。
Zhēn shì sě xiāng wèi jù quán a.

● I cooked this dish myself. Please have a taste.
● It's delicious.

这是我做的 _____，请您
zhè shì wǒ zuò de 　　　　 qǐng nín
尝尝吧。
chángchang ba

饭
fàn
rice

小吃
xiǎochī
snack

饺子
jiǎozi
dumpling

NOTES

When Chinese people intend to invite friends to their home for dinner, they usually spend a lot of time preparing. They clean their house and prepare sumptuous food and drink. When Chinese people go to visit others, they bring gifts such as fruits.

36

我 们 该 告 辞 了 。
Wǒmen gāi gàocí le.

It's time to say goodbye.

● 时间不早了，我们该告辞了。
Shíjiān bù zǎo le, wǒmen gāi gàocí le.

● 再坐会儿吧。
Zài zuò huìr ba.

● It's quite late. It's time to say goodbye.
● Please stay a bit longer.

我们该＿＿＿＿了。
wǒmen gāi ＿＿＿ le

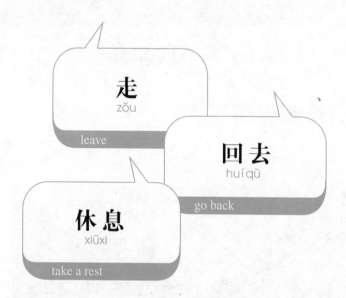

走
zǒu
leave

回去
huíqù
go back

休息
xiūxi
take a rest

NOTES

When you want to visit a Chinese family, it's best to make an appointment. Unless you are invited for a meal, you should try to avoid visiting during mealtimes. When you do go to visit, you should prepare some kind of gift, and you should not stay for too long. Not very long after the meal or tea, you should bid the host/hostess goodbye.

37

您家的客厅真漂亮！
Nín jiā de kètīng zhēn piǎoliang!

You've got a beautiful living room!

● 您家的客厅真漂亮！
Nín jiā de kètīng zhēn piǎoliang!

● 哪里哪里。
Nǎlǐ nǎlǐ.

● You've got a beautiful living room!
● Well, you flatter me.

_____真漂亮！
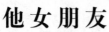
zhēn piǎoliang

他女朋友
tā nǚpéngyou

his girlfriend

你女儿
nǐ nǚ'ér

your daughter

你的手机
nǐ de shǒujī

your cell phone

In China, polite expressions help create a harmonious atmosphere. These expressions convey formality and modesty. Yet along with the development of society, the language people use has become more and more modern. For example, in the past, when people were praised by others, they tended to say: "Nǎlǐ nǎlǐ.(You flatter me!)" Now, people often say "Xièxie. (Thank you.)" instead.

38

我今天晚上过得特别高兴。
Wǒ jīntiān wǎnshang guò de tèbié gāoxìng.

I've had a wonderful time this evening.

● 谢谢你的招待，我今天
Xièxie nǐ de zhāodài, wǒ jīntiān

晚上过得特别高兴。
wǎnshang guò de tèbié gāoxìng.

● 有空儿常来啊。
Yǒu kòngr cháng lái a.

● Thanks for your hospitality. I've had a wonderful time this evening.

● Please do come visit again.

我今天晚上过得特别_____。
wǒ jīntiān wǎnshang guò de tèbié

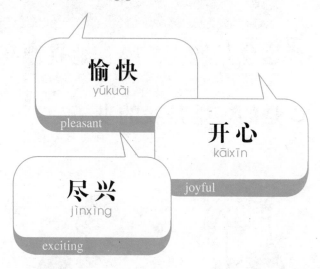

愉快
yúkuài
pleasant

开心
kāixīn
joyful

尽兴
jìnxìng
exciting

NOTES

When you pay a visit to your friend's house, the host/hostess will often say words such as: huānyíng (welcome); kuài qǐngjìn (please come in); qǐng mànyòng chá / fàncài (please take your time to enjoy the tea/meal); nín mànzǒu (please mind your step); yǒu kòng cháng lái wán (please do come visit us again), etc. The guest will often reply with words such as: xièxie nǐmen de rèqíng zhāodài (thank you for your hospitality); shíhou bù zǎo le, wǒmen gāi gàocí le (it's quite late and it's time to say goodbye); qǐng liúbù (don't bother to see me off any further).

39

这 位 是 您 夫 人 吗 ？
Zhè wèi shì nín fūrén ma?

Is this your wife?

● 这位是您夫人吗？她真漂亮。
Zhè wèi shì nín fūrén ma? Tā zhēn piàoliang.

● 是的，她是我的妻子。
Shìde, tā shì wǒ de qīzi.

● Is this your wife? She is really beautiful.
● Yes, she is my wife.

这位是您＿＿＿吗？
zhè wèi shì nín ＿＿＿ ma

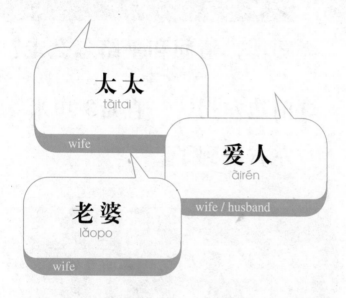

太太
tàitai

wife

爱人
àirén

wife / husband

老婆
lǎopo

wife

NOTES

Nowadays, a man often calls his wife "lǎopo, qīzi, àirén, fūrén, nèirén, etc". A woman calls her husband "lǎogōng, zhàngfu, àirén, etc".

40

师傅，请问和平路怎么走？
Shīfu, qǐngwèn Hépíng Lù zěnme zǒu?

Excuse me, how do I get to Heping Road?

● 师傅，请问和平路怎么走？
Shīfu, qǐngwèn Hépíng Lù zěnme zǒu?

● 前边左拐，一直走300米
Qiánbian zuǒ guǎi, yìzhí zǒu sānbǎi mǐ

左右就到了。
zuǒyòu jiù dào le.

○ Excuse me, how do I get to Heping Road?

○ Go along the street and turn left, then walk about 300 meters and there you are.

＿＿＿＿，请问和平路怎么走？
qǐngwèn Hépíng Lù　zěnme zǒu

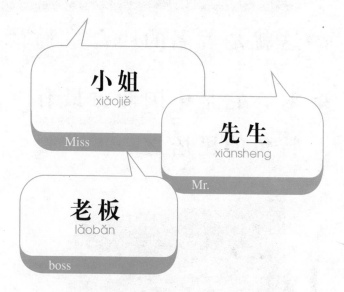

小姐
xiǎojiě

Miss

先生
xiānsheng

Mr.

老板
lǎobǎn

boss

NOTES

In daily conversation, people often address an employee as "shīfu (master)" who works in a shop, in the service industry or in the travel industry. "Xiǎojiě" (Miss) originally referred to unmarried ladies of noble social status, but now it is used commonly to address young women.

41

这就是著名的四合院吗？
Zhè jiù shì zhùmíng de sìhéyuàn ma?

Is this a well-known siheyuan courtyard?

● 这就是著名的四合院吗？
Zhè jiù shì zhùmíng de sìhéyuàn ma?

● 对，它是中国北方最有
Duì, tā shì Zhōngguó běifāng zuì yǒu

特色的民居之一。
tèsè de mínjū zhī yī.

● Is this a well-known siheyuàn courtyard?

● Yes, it is. This is the most characteristic dwelling in North China.

82

这就是著名的_____吗？
zhè jiù shì zhùmíng de _____ ma

万里长城
Wànlǐ Chángchéng

the Great Wall

北京烤鸭
Běijīng kǎoyā

Beijing roast duck

壶口瀑布
Húkǒu Pùbù

Hukou waterfall

NOTES

A siheyuan courtyard is usually composed of the principal room (usually the north room), the wing rooms along the east and west sides, and the south room, surrounding a courtyard. Along the principal rooms, small rooms are sometimes built on each side. There are corridors connecting the rooms on four sides and giving shelter in rainy weather.

42

怪不得它叫"四合院"呢。

Guàibude tā jiào "sìhéyuàn" ne.

No wonder it is called a four-section courtyard (siheyuan courtyard).

● 一个院子、四面有房，怪不得
Yí gè yuànzi, sì miàn yǒu fáng, guàibude

它叫"四合院"呢。
tā jiào "sìhéyuàn" ne.

● 看来你看明白了。
Kànlái nǐ kàn míngbai le.

● It's a courtyard that is surrounded with rooms on four sides. No wonder it is called a four-section courtyard (siheyuan courtyard).

● Now you understand.

怪不得_____呢。
guàibude _____ ne

你喜欢他
nǐ xǐhuan tā

You like him.

你不爱吃饺子
nǐ bú ài chī jiǎozi

You do not like to eat dumplings.

房间里这么凉快
fángjiān li zhème liángkuai

The room is so cool.

> **NOTES**
>
> Generally, a siheyuan courtyard has two courtyards. The big-sized compounds have three or four courtyards, in addition to a garden. The two courtyards are divided by a wall that goes from the east wing room to the west wing room. The outer courtyard is enclosed by the dwellings for the workers. The inner courtyard is encompassed by the dwellings for the master and his family. The main gate facing the street is comparatively simple and usually built on the left side.

43

这座房子有多少年的历史了？

Zhè zuò fángzi yǒu duōshao nián de lìshǐ le?

How long has it been since the house was built?

● 这座房子有多少年的历史了？

　　Zhè zuò fángzi yǒu duōshao nián de lìshǐ le?

● 这座房子有700年的历史了。

　　Zhè zuò fángzi yǒu qībǎi nián de lìshǐ le.

○ How long has it been since the house was built?

● It has been 700 years since the house was built.

_____有多少年的历史了？
yǒu duōshao nián de lìshǐ le

中国文化
Zhōngguó wénhuà

Chinese culture

新中国
xīn Zhōngguó

the New China

天坛
Tiāntán

the Temple of Heaven

NOTES

In China, dwellings take different forms in accordance with different geographic environments and different nationalities. For example, the siheyuan courtyard is a typical compound in the countryside of North China. In the South, however, architectural styles are more varied and free. People of Han nationality live in brick and tile buildings, such as the siheyuan courtyard, while the minorities have their own architectural styles. For instance, the Dais live in bamboo buildings, the Miaos live in "diaojiaolou (a kind of wooden or bamboo house in mountainous areas that is supported by wooden stakes, and accessed by a ladder)", and the Mongolians live in yurts.

44

我想这是北方建筑风格吧？

Wǒ xiǎng zhè shì běifāng jiànzhù fēnggé ba?

I think this kind of architectural style belongs to North China, doesn't it?

● **我想这是北方建筑风格吧？**

Wǒ xiǎng zhè shì běifāng jiànzhù fēnggé ba?

● **不错，中国南方和北方的**

Búcuò, Zhōngguó nánfāng hé běifāng de

建筑风格差别特别大。

jiànzhù fēnggé chābié tèbié dà.

◐ I think this kind of architectural style belongs to North China, doesn't it?

◑ Yes, indeed. The architectural styles in the North differ greatly from those in the South.

我想这是_____建筑风格吧？
wǒ xiǎng zhè shì   jiànzhù fēnggé ba

中国
Zhōngguó

Chinese

哥特式
Gētèshì

Gothic

巴洛克
Bāluòkè

Baroque

NOTES

The siheyuan courtyard in North China, cave dwellings in Shanxi and Shaanxi Provinces, yurts in Inner Mongolia, felt tents in Xinjiang, rammed-earth houses in Kashgar, mountainous dwellings in Lijiang, dwellings of the Bai nationality in Dali, and Diaojiaolou in the west of Hunan Province… all these are among the various architectural styles of Chinese buildings that have been developed in accordance with the local climate and geographic conditions.

45

长城是一定要去的地方吗？

Chángchéng shì yídìng yào qù de dìfang ma?

The Great Wall is a place that one should not miss, isn't it?

● 对外国人来说，长城是
Duì wàiguórén lái shuō, Chángchéng shì

一定要去的地方吗？
yídìng yào qù de dìfang ma?

● 没错，"不到长城非好汉"嘛。
Méicuò, "bú dào Chángchéng fēi hǎo hàn" ma.

● For foreigners, the Great Wall is a place that one should not miss, isn't it?

● Yes, absolutely. As the saying goes: "If you haven't reached the Great Wall, you're not a real man".

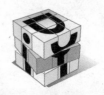

＿＿＿是一定要去的地方吗?
shì yídìng yào qù de dìfang ma

北京
Běijīng

Beijing

巴黎
Bālí

Paris

纽约
Niǔyuē

New York

NOTES

The Great Wall, which stretches across a vast expanse of land in the northern and central China, reaches a total length of 6,700 kilometers. It is the most spectacular military defense fortification in ancient China. "If you haven't reached the Great Wall, you're not a real man" only means that one will not be called as a real man unless he has been to the Great Wall.

46

你可以给我介绍一下长城的历史吗?

Nǐ kěyǐ gěi wǒ jièshào yíxià Chángchéng de lìshǐ ma?

Would you please tell us about the history of the Great Wall?

○ 你可以给我介绍一下长城
Nǐ kěyǐ gěi wǒ jièshào yíxià Chángchéng

的历史吗?
de lìshǐ ma?

○ 长城有2000多年的历史了。
Chángchéng yǒu liǎngqiān duō nián de lìshǐ le.

○ Would you please tell us about the history of the Great Wall?

○ The Great Wall has had a history of more than 2000 years.

你可以给我介绍一下＿＿＿的
Nǐ kěyǐ gěi wǒ jièshào yíxià de

历史吗？
lìshǐ ma

故宫
Gùgōng

the Forbidden City

金字塔
jīnzìtǎ

the pyramid

比萨斜塔
Bǐsà Xiétǎ

the Leaning Tower of Pisa

NOTES

Ever since the 7th or 8th century B.C., the Great Wall had been under constant construction for 2,000 years. It's total length reaches 6,700 kilometers. It has been ranked as one of the seven wonders of the Middle Ages, along with the Colosseum of Rome and the Leaning Tower of Pisa.

47

现在中国学生还学"四书五经"吗？
Xiànzài Zhōngguó xuésheng hái xué "sìshū wǔjīng" ma?

Do students in China still learn the "Four Books and Five Classics"?

● 现在中国学生还学"四书
Xiànzài Zhōngguó xuésheng hái xué "sìshū

五经"吗？
wǔjīng" ma?

● 学是学，可学的目的、
Xuéshìxué, kě xué de mùdì,

方法不同了。
fāngfǎ bù tóng le.

○ Do students in China still learn the "Four Books and Five Classics"?

● Learn as they might, but the purpose of learning these classics and their methods are quite different.

现在中国学生还学

xiànzài Zhōngguó xuésheng hái xué

_____ 吗？

ma

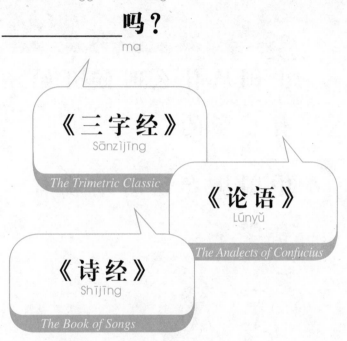

《三字经》
Sānzìjīng

The Trimetric Classic

《论语》
Lúnyǔ

The Analects of Confucius

《诗经》
Shījīng

The Book of Songs

NOTES

   "The Four Books" refer to *The Great Learning, The Doctrine of the Mean, The Analects of Confucius,* and *The Mencius.* "The Five Classics" are, namely, *The Book of Changes, Classic of Documents, The Book of Songs, The Book of Rites,* and *The Spring and Autumn Annals.* All of these are authoritative books of Confucianism, and also the basis of study for civil service examinations in China.

48

中国从什么时候开始有私学的？
Zhōngguó cóng shénme shíhou kāishǐ yǒu sīxué de?

When did China begin to have private schools?

○ **中国从什么时候开始**
Zhōngguó cóng shénme shíhou kāishǐ

有私学的？
yǒu sīxué de?

● **中国从春秋时期就有**
Zhōngguó cóng Chūnqiū shíqī jiù yǒu

私学了。
sīxué le.

○ When did China begin to have private schools?

● The first private schools in China can date back to the Spring and Autumn Period.

中国从什么时候开始
Zhōngguó cóng shénme shíhou kāishǐ

有 _____ 的？
yǒu de

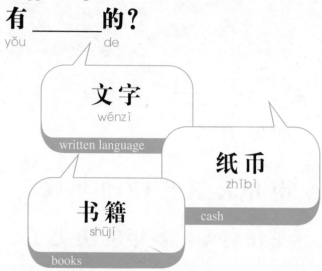

文字
wénzì
written language

纸币
zhǐbì
cash

书籍
shūjí
books

In the Western Zhou Dynasty, education in China was controlled by the government, that is to say, access to culture and education was reserved for aristocrats only. Confucius was the first educator in history to set up a private school. From then on, people from lower social ranks began to gain access to education. After Confucius, Mozi and Mencius set up private schools as well. They all made important contributions to Chinese culture and education. In the Song Dynasty, academies of classical learning began to spread far and wide, signifying the climax of private schools in China. Currently, schools and colleges sponsored by private funds are still an important part of Chinese education.

49

南开大学有80多年的历史了吧?

Nánkāi Dàxué yǒu bāshí duō nián de lìshǐ le ba?

Nankai University has a history of over eighty years, doesn't it?

● 南开大学有80多年的
Nánkāi Dàxué yǒu bāshí duō nián de

历史了吧?
lìshǐ le ba?

● 南开大学于1919年成立,
Nánkāi Dàxué yú yījiǔyījiǔ nián chénglì,

现在有80多年的历史了。
xiànzài yǒu bāshí duō nián de lìshǐ le.

● Nankai University has a history of over eighty years, doesn't it?

● Nankai University was founded in 1919. It has a history of over eighty years.

_____有_____了吧？
　　　yǒu　　　　　le ba

李叔叔　四十岁
Lǐ shūshu　sìshí suì
Uncle Li　in his forties

班里　有六十个学生
bān li　yǒu liùshí gè xuésheng
in the class　there are 60 students

NOTES

Nankai University was originally sponsored by private funds. It was founded in 1919 by two well-known patriotic educators, Zhang Boling and Yan Xiu. Nankai University is now one of the most comprehensive, research-oriented universities in China and incorporates all disciplines of learning. Zhou Enlai, the first premier of the PRC, was once a student at Nankai University.

50

咱们什么时候也去参观一下北大、清华吧？

Zánmen shénme shíhou yě qù cānguān yíxià Běidà, Qīnghuá ba?

Let's go and visit Peking University and Tsinghua University someday!

● **咱们什么时候也去参观一下**
Zánmen shénme shíhou yě qù cānguān yíxià

北大、清华吧？
Běidà, Qīnghuá ba?

● **好啊，我给你当导游。**
Hǎo a, wǒ gěi nǐ dāng dǎoyóu.

● Let's go and visit Peking University and Tsinghua University someday!

● A wonderful idea! I can be your tour guide.

咱们什么时候也去_____吧？
zánmen shénme shíhou yě qù _____ ba

逛商场
guàng shāngchǎng

go shopping

听相声
tīng xiàngsheng

listen to Chinese cross-talk

学开车
xué kāichē

learn to drive

Peking University and Tsinghua University are the two most famous universities in China. Both are located in Beijing, the capital of China. It is generally believed that Peking University is known for its humanity studies and Tsinghua University for its science and engineering studies. Since both of the universities are among the top-ranked schools in China, each has its own special scenes and sights of cultural interests, having developed a distinctive university culture. They have become tour sights for many tourists in recent years.

51

我看你还是报中文系吧。

Wǒ kàn nǐ háishi bào zhōngwénxì ba.

I think that you may choose the Chinese Department as well.

● 你看我学哪个专业好？

Nǐ kàn wǒ xué nǎge zhuānyè hǎo?

● 我看你还是报中文系吧，

Wǒ kàn nǐ háishi bào zhōngwénxì ba,

中文系的课挺有意思的。

zhōngwénxì de kè tǐng yǒuyìsi de.

○ What major do you think I should choose?

● I think that you may choose the Chinese Department as well, as the courses offered by the Chinese Department are quite interesting.

我看你还是报＿＿＿＿吧。

wǒ kàn nǐ háishi bào ba

> **历史系**
> lìshǐxì
> the History Department

> **外语系**
> wàiyǔxì
> the Foreign Language Department

> **数学系**
> shùxuéxì
> the Mathematics Department

NOTES

China has promulgated a nine-year compulsory education system, such that children are required to attend six years of primary education and three years of junior high school education. After nine years of compulsory education, students may choose to go into vocational schools or enter high schools. The high school education also lasts for three years. After graduating from high schools, students are free to choose a major and university for further study (for example, science, engineering, medicine, economics, management, humanity, law, art, etc).

52

中文系的课容易学吗？
Zhōngwénxì de kè róngyì xué ma?

Are the courses in the Chinese Department easy?

● 中文系的课容易学吗？
Zhōngwénxì de kè róngyì xué ma?

● 既然你那么热爱中国文化，
Jìrán nǐ nàme rè'ài Zhōngguó wénhuà,

就一定能够学好。
jiù yídìng nénggòu xué hǎo.

● Are the courses in the Chinese Department easy?
● Now that you have such a keen interest in Chinese culture, you will surely be able to manage the courses well.

＿＿＿＿容易学吗？
róngyì xué ma

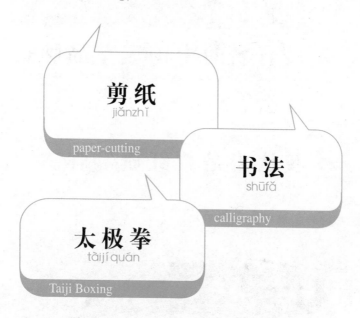

剪纸
jiǎnzhǐ

paper-cutting

书法
shūfǎ

calligraphy

太极拳
tàijíquán

Taiji Boxing

NOTES

Generally speaking, the courses offered in Chinese Department in China's universities cover two major disciplines: linguistics and literature. In some universities, however, they offer courses in art and communication as well.

53

最有名的中国汽车品牌是什么？
Zuì yǒumíng de Zhōngguó qìchē pīnpái shì shénme?

What's the most famous car brand in China?

- 最有名的中国汽车品牌是
  Zuì yǒumíng de Zhōngguó qìchē pīnpái shì

  什么？
  shénme?

- 我认为是"红旗"牌。
  Wǒ rènwéi shì "Hóngqí" Pái.

- What's the most famous car brand in China?
- It's "Hongqi (Red Flag)."

106

最有名的中国_____品牌是
zuì yǒumíng de Zhōngguó pǐnpái shì

什么?
shénme

电视
diànshì

TV set

化妆品
huàzhuāngpǐn

cosmetics

方便面
fāngbiànmiàn

instant noodles

NOTES

In China, the "Honqi (Red Flag)" brand car is known by everyone. The history of "Honqi (Red Flag)" dates back to 1958. It was the first car developed wholly by Chinese designers and engineers. In the last twenty years, China's automobile industry has developed rapidly, and as a result, there are more and more famous car brands.

54

开私家车的人越来越多了。

Kāi sījiāchē de rén yuèláiyuè duō le.

More and more people own private cars nowadays.

开私家车的人越来越多了。

Kāi sījiāchē de rén yuèláiyuè duō le.

是啊。

'Shì a.

More and more people own private cars nowadays.

Yes, indeed.

_____的人越来越多了。
de rén yuèláiyuè duō le

学英语
xué Yīngyǔ

learn English

买汽车
mǎi qìchē

buy cars

旅行结婚
lǚxíng jiéhūn

have a honeymoon trip

NOTES

China FAW Group Corporation started work on July 15th, 1953, and Chairman Mao Zedong wrote the epigraph "memorial for the foundation of the First Automobile Factory". The automobile industry of New China was launched at that time. On July 13th, 1956, the first truck made in China went down the assembly line, signifying an end to the time when China was not able to make automobiles. In recent decades, China's automobile industry has made rapid development.

55

哪件唐装最漂亮？

Nǎ   jiàn   tángzhuāng   zuì   piàoliang?

Which Tangzhuang (Chinese-style dress) is the most beautiful one?

● **哪件 唐装 最漂亮？**
　Nǎ jiàn tángzhuāng zuì piàoliang?

● **很难说，它们各有各的**
　Hěn nán shuō,　tāmen gè yǒu gè de
　特点。
　tèdiǎn.

○ Which Tangzhuang (Chinese-style dress) is the most
　beautiful one?

● It's hard to say. Each has its own characteristics.

哪件_____最漂亮?
nǎ jiàn　　　　　zuì piàoliang

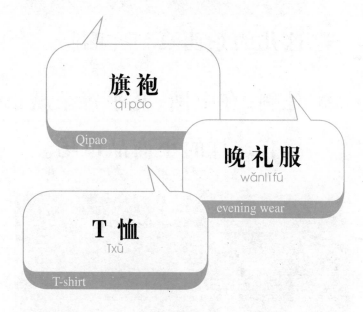

旗袍
qípáo

Qipao

晚礼服
wǎnlǐfú

evening wear

T 恤
Txù

T-shirt

"Tangzhuang", is a kind of Chinese style dress evolved from the Manchu jacket of the Qing Dynasty. The term "Tangzhuang" is so named because foreigners often called the "Chinese Street" as "Tangrenjie (China Town)", and so accordingly, they called the Chinese style dress as "Tangzhuang".

56

这儿的东西真便宜啊！
Zhèr de dōngxi zhēn piányi a!

The things sold here are really cheap!

○ **这儿的东西真便宜啊！**
Zhèr de dōngxi zhēn piányi a!

● **是啊。在中国，几乎每个城市**
Shì a. Zài Zhōngguó, jīhū měi gè chéngshì

都有这样的小商品市场。
dōu yǒu zhèyàng de xiǎo shāngpǐn shìchǎng.

○ The things sold here are really cheap!

● Yes, indeed. In almost every city in China, you will find small commodity markets like this one.

这儿的东西真_____啊！
zhèr de dōngxi zhēn a

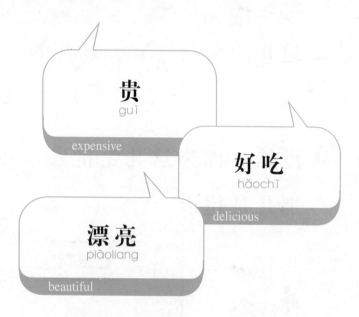

贵
guì

expensive

好吃
hǎochī

delicious

漂亮
piàoliang

beautiful

NOTES

In the last twenty years, the Chinese economy, and the small commodity industry in particular, has made rapid development. Take, for example, a small town called Yiwu in Zhejiang Province: every small commodity businessman knows that he can find the cheapest and most complete assortment of products there.

57

这儿的东西便宜，那儿的东西贵。
Zhèr de dōngxi piányi, nǎr de dōngxi guì.

The goods sold here are cheap, while the goods sold there are expensive.

● 这儿的东西便宜，那儿的
Zhèr de dōngxi piányi, nǎr de

东西贵。
dōngxi guì.

● 没错，因为这儿是批发市场，
Méicuò, yīnwèi zhèr shì pīfā shìchǎng,

那儿是超市。
nǎr shì chāoshì.

×× 超市

● The goods sold here are cheap, while the goods sold there are expensive.

● Yes, exactly. This is a wholesale market, and that is a supermarket.

这儿的 _____，那儿的 _____。
zhèr de   nàr de

天气冷　天气热
tiānqì lěng   tiānqì rè

the weather is cold   the weather is warm

水果新鲜　水果不新鲜
shuǐguǒ xīnxiān   shuǐguǒ bù xīnxiān

the fruits are fresh   the fruits are not fresh

NOTES

In a wholesale market, you can bargain with the shopkeepers. So, very often you can buy commodities in excellent quality and reasonable price. The same assortment of small commodities sold in a supermarket are labeled with set prices, so, generally speaking, they are slightly higher priced.

58

你连秦始皇都不知道？
Nǐ lián Qínshǐhuáng dōu bù zhīdào?

You do not even know Qinshihuang?

● **你连秦始皇都不知道？**
Nǐ lián Qínshǐhuáng dōu bù zhīdào?

● **那你给我介绍介绍吧。**
Nà nǐ gěi wǒ jièshào jièshào ba.

○ You do not even know Qinshihuang (the first emperor of a united China)?

◐ No, so tell me something about him.

你连＿＿＿＿＿都不知道？
nǐ lián　　　　　　　　　dōu bù zhīdào

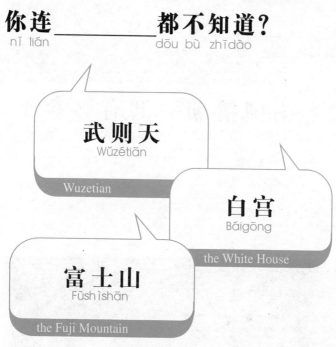

武则天
Wǔzétiān

Wuzetian

白宫
Báigōng

the White House

富士山
Fùshìshān

the Fuji Mountain

Qinshihuang, born as Ying Zheng, was the first emperor of a united China. In 221 B.C., he unified China into one country and set new models and regulations to unify the way of writing Chinese characters, the measures for length and for weight, the design of currency, and the width of cart axles. Emperor Qinshihuang succeeded in joining together lengths of the Great Wall to fend off invasions from the Huns in the north after the unification of China.

59

中国清朝一共有多少个皇帝？

Zhōngguó Qīngcháo yígòng yǒu duōshao gè huángdì?

How many emperors were there in the Qing Dynasty?

● 中国清朝一共有多少个

Zhōngguó Qīngcháo yígòng yǒu duōshao gè

皇帝？

huángdì?

● 12个。

Shí'èr gè.

● How many emperors were there in the Qing Dynasty?

● Twelve.

中国一共有多少个 _____？

Zhōngguó yí gòng yǒu duōshao gè

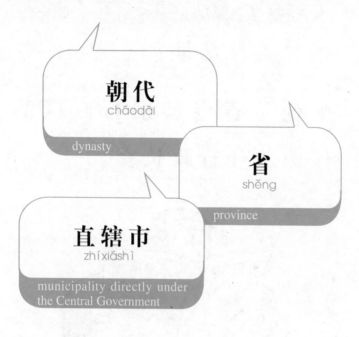

朝代
cháodài
dynasty

省
shěng
province

直辖市
zhíxiáshì
municipality directly under
the Central Government

NOTES

The Qing Dynasty (1616–1911) was founded by a minority ethnic people, the Manchus. The Kuomingtang led by Sun Yat-sen overthrew the ruling of the Qing Dynasty and founded the Republic of China in 1911. Since the Qing Dynasty was the last feudal dynasty in China, the last emperor of the Qing Dynasty is often addressed as "mòdài huángdì" (the last emperor).

60

曾 荫 权 是 谁？
Zēng　Yìnquán　shì　shuí?

Who is Mr. Donald Tsang Yam-kuen?

● **曾 荫 权 是 谁？**
Zēng Yìnquán shì shuí?

● **他 是 香 港 特 别 行 政 区 的**
Tā　shì　Xiānggǎng　tèbié　xíngzhèng qū　de

第 二 任 行 政 长 官。
dì'èr　rèn xíngzhèng zhǎngguān.

● Who is Mr. Donald Tsang Yam-kuen?

● He is the second Chief Executive of the Hong Kong
Special Administrative Region.

_____是谁？
shì shuí

毛泽东
Máo Zédōng

Mao Zedong

周恩来
Zhōu Ēnlái

Zhou Enlai

林肯
Línkěn

Abraham Lincoln

NOTES

At present, China has set up two special administrative regions. The Hong·Kong Special Administrative Region was founded on July 1st, 1997. Its first Chief Executive is Mr. Tung Chee-hwa, and the second is Mr. Donald Tsang Yam-kuen. The Macao Special Administrative Region was founded on December 20th, 1999, and its first Chief Executive is Mr. Edmund Ho.

61

周恩来先生是干什么的？
Zhōu Ēnlái xiānsheng shì gàn shénme de?

Who was Mr. Zhou Enlai?

● 周恩来先生是干什么的？
Zhōu Ēnlái xiānsheng shì gàn shénme de?

● 他曾经是中国的总理。
Tā céngjīng shì Zhōngguó de zǒnglǐ.

● Who was Mr. Zhou Enlai?
● He was once the premier of the People's Republic of China.

_____是干什么的？
shì gàn shénme de

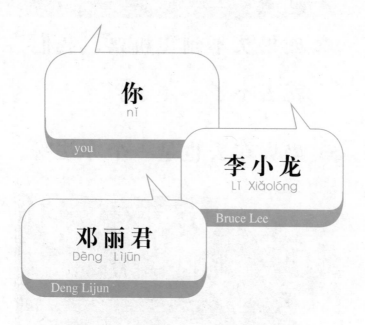

你
nǐ

you

李 小 龙
Lǐ Xiǎolóng

Bruce Lee

邓 丽 君
Dèng Lìjūn

Deng Lijun

NOTES

Mr. Zhou Enlai was the first premier of the People's Republic of China. Currently Mr. Wen Jiabao is the premier. The first chairman of the PRC was Mao Zedong, and at present, Hu Jintao is the chairman.

62

如果买不到飞机票，我们就去不了西藏了。

Rúguǒ mǎi bú dào fēijī piào, wǒmen jiù qùbuliǎo Xīzàng le.

If flight tickets are not available, then we cannot go to Tibet.

如果买不到飞机票，我们
Rúguǒ mǎi bú dào fēijī piào, wǒmen

就去不了西藏了。
jiù qùbuliǎo Xīzàng le.

坐火车去也是一个办法呀。
Zuò huǒchē qù yě shì yí gè bànfǎ ya.

- If flight tickets are not available, then we cannot go to Tibet.
- Going by train is an alternative.

如果买不到飞机票，我们就
rúguǒ mǎi bú dào fēijī piào wǒmen jiù
去不了＿＿＿＿了。
qùbuliǎo le

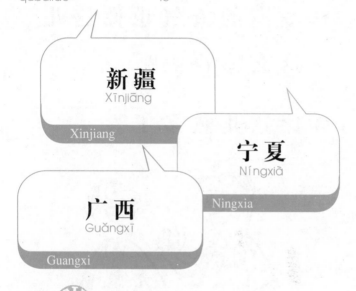

新疆
Xīnjiāng
Xinjiang

宁夏
Níngxià
Ningxia

广西
Guǎngxī
Guangxi

China's administrative units are currently based on a three-tier system, dividing the nation into provinces, counties and townships. A province or an autonomous region is subdivided into autonomous prefectures, counties, autonomous counties and/or cities. A county or an autonomous county is subdivided into townships, ethnic townships and/or towns. Tibet is known as the Tibet Autonomous Region of China.

63

香港的天气也像这儿这么凉快吗?

Xiānggǎng de tiānqì yě xiàng zhèr zhème liángkuai ma?

Is the weather in Hong Kong as cool as here?

● 香港 的 天气 也 像 这儿
Xiānggǎng de tiānqì yě xiàng zhèr

这么 凉快 吗?
zhème liángkuai ma?

● 比 这儿 热 多 了。
Bǐ zhèr rè duō le.

○ Is the weather in Hong Kong as cool as here?
● The weather there is much warmer.

＿＿＿的天气也像这儿这么
de tiānqì yě xiàng zhèr zhème

凉快吗？
liángkuai ma

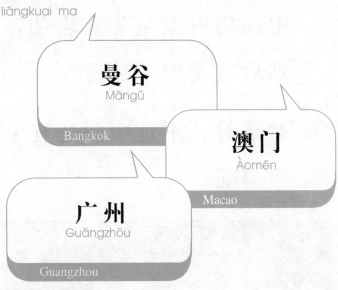

曼谷
Mǎngǔ

Bangkok

澳门
Àomén

Macao

广州
Guǎngzhōu

Guangzhou

NOTES

Hong Kong is a Special Autonomous Region of China (HKSAR). It is governed under the policy "one county, two systems". Unlike the other provinces and autonomous regions, the HKSAR enjoys a high degree of autonomy except in defense and foreign affairs. The HKSAR exercises executive, legislative and independent judicial power, including that of final adjudication.

127

64

对是对，不过中间还有个宋朝呢

Duìshiduì, búguò zhōngjiān hái yǒu gè Sòngchāo ne.

Yes, you are right, but the Song Dynasty comes between the two.

● **中国历史上是先有唐朝，**
　Zhōngguó lìshǐ shang shì xiān yǒu Tángchāo,

然后有元朝，对吗？
ránhòu yǒu Yuánchāo, duì ma?

● **对是对，不过中间还有个**
　Duìshiduì, búguò zhōngjiān hái yǒu gè

宋朝呢。
Sòngchāo ne.

● Is it true that the Tang Dynasty comes before the Yuan Dynasty in Chinese history?

● Yes, you are right, but the Song Dynasty comes between the two.

对是对，不过中间还有个

duìshìduì　bùguǒ zhōngjiān hái yǒu gè

＿＿＿呢。

ne

商 朝
Shāngcháo

Shang Dynasty

周 朝
Zhōucháo

Zhou Dynasty

清 朝
Qīngcháo

Qing Dynasty

NOTES

The Tang Dynasty (618–907), with its capital at Chang'an, is regarded by historians as a high point in Chinese civilization — equal, or even superior, to the Han Dynasty. Stimulated by contact with India and the Middle East, the empire saw a flowering of creativity in many fields, such as block printing, civil service examination, literature and art, etc.

65

电视里正在演唐太宗的故事呢

Diànshì li zhēngzài yǎn Tángtàizōng de gùshi ne!

The story of Tangtaizong is on TV now!

● 看！电视里正在演唐太宗
Kàn! Diànshì li zhēngzài yǎn Tángtàizōng

的故事呢！
de gùshi ne!

● 这是历史上著名的"贞观
Zhè shì lìshǐ shang zhùmíng de "Zhēnguān

之治"。
Zhīzhì".

● Look! The story of Tangtaizong is on TV now!
● It's about the well-known period in Chinese history
known as "the Well-Managed Zhenguan Reign".

电视里正在演_____的故事呢！

diànshì li zhèngzài yǎn _____ de gùshi ne

末代皇帝

mòdài huángdì

the last emperor

汉武帝

Hànwǔdì

Hanwudi

慈禧

Cíxǐ

Cixi

NOTES

Some of the great imperial monarchs in Chinese history are Qinshihuang, Hangaozu, Hanwudi, Suiwendi, Tangtaizu, Tangxuanzong, Songtaizu, Genghis Khan, Kublai Khan, Kangxi, and Qianlong. They all made contributions to the development of Chinese history, since some of them governed the country with the policy of benevolence, some accepted advice easily, and others carried out reforms.

131

66

听说毛泽东不但是政治家，还是个诗人。
Tīngshuō Máo Zédōng búdàn shì zhèngzhìjiā, hái shì gè shīrén.

I hear that Mao Zedong was not only a statesman, but a poet as well.

● 听说毛泽东不但是政治家，
Tīngshuō Máo Zédōng búdàn shì zhèngzhìjiā,

还是个诗人。
hái shì gè shīrén.

● 是啊，他有一句很著名的
Shì a, tā yǒu yí jù hěn zhùmíng de

诗："数风流人物,还看今朝"。
shī: "shǔ fēngliú rénwù, hái kàn jīnzhāo".

● I hear that Mao Zedong was not only a statesman, but a poet as well.

● Yes, indeed. A famous stanza from one of his poems is: "All are past and gone! For truly great men, look to this age alone."

听说他不但＿＿＿，还＿＿＿。
tīngshuō tā búdàn hái

会说英语　会说法语
huì shuō Yīngyǔ　huì shuō Fǎyǔ

can speak English　can speak French

来过亚洲　去过非洲
láiguo Yàzhōu　qùguo Fēizhōu

has been to Asia　has been to Africa

Many well-known figures in Chinese history had versatile talents. Take, for example, the powerful and ambitious figure of the late Eastern Han Dynasty, Cao Cao, who not only unified the northern territory of China, but also wrote many poems that are still popular today. Verses such as: "Duì jiǔ dāng gē, rénshēng jǐhé. (Here before us, wine and song! For man does not live long.)", and "Lǎojì fúlì, zhì zài qiānlǐ. (An old war-horse may be stabled, yet still it longs to gallop a thousand li.)" still enjoy great use in daily communications.

67

我要去西安了！
Wǒ yào qù Xī'ān le!

I'm leaving for Xi'an.

● 我要去西安了！
Wǒ yào qù Xī'ān le!

● 那你一定要去看兵马俑呀。
Nà nǐ yídìng yào qù kàn bīngmǎyǒng ya.

● I'm leaving for Xi'an.

● Then don't forget to visit the terracotta warriors and horses.

我要去＿＿＿了！
wǒ yào qù　　　　le

南京
Nánjīng

Nanjing

威尼斯
Wēinísī

Venice

伦敦
Lúndūn

London

NOTES

The mausoleum of the first emperor of China, Qinshihuang, was constructed to mimic the design of the capital city of the Qin Dynasty. The terracotta warriors and horses, which symbolize his Majesty's spectacular underground troops, were buried in the funerary pits. There are more than seven thousand terracotta warriors and horses in the pits, which are lined up in a practical battle formation. This archaeological find has become known as "the eighth wonder of the world".

68

平遥古城在哪个省？
Píngyáo gǔchéng zài nǎge shěng?

Which province is Pingyao in?

● 平遥古城在哪个省？
Píngyáo gǔchéng zài nǎge shěng?

● 在山西省。
Zài Shānxī Shěng.

● Which province is Pingyao in?
● It's in Shanxi province.

_____在哪个省?
zài nǎge shěng

九寨沟
Jiǔzhàigōu

Jiuzhaigou

张家界
Zhāngjiājiè

Zhangjiajie

西湖
Xīhú

the West Lake

NOTES

Pingyao is a small town that lies in central Shanxi Province. Even now, the walls, streets, dwellings, shops and temples remain much the same as when they were constructed, giving us a chance to see the layout and style of the architecture of ancient China. On December 3rd 1997, Pingyao was listed on the *World Heritage List*.

69

我这里有几张京剧票，走，一起看戏去
Wǒ zhèlǐ yǒu jǐ zhāng jīngjù piào, zǒu, yìqǐ kàn xì qu.

I've got a few tickets for Peking opera. Let's go and watch a play.

● 我这里有几张京剧票，走，
Wǒ zhèlǐ yǒu jǐ zhāng jīngjù piào, zǒu,

一起看戏去。
yìqǐ kàn xì qu.

● 我正好闲着，太棒了！
Wǒ zhènghǎo xián zhe, tài bàng le!

● I've got a few tickets for Peking Opera. Let's go and watch a play.

● Terrific! I have free time.

走，一起_____去。
zǒu　yìqǐ　　　　qù

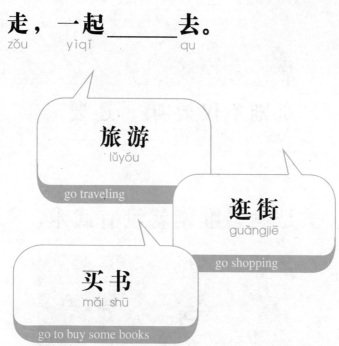

旅游
lǚyóu

go traveling

逛街
guàngjiē

go shopping

买书
mǎi shū

go to buy some books

NOTES

Peking opera was born when Anhui troupes came to Beijing. Among these troupes, which came to Beijng in the Qing Dynasty, were the Four Great Anhui Troupes, namely, Sanqing, Sixi, Chuntai and Hechun. When they performed on stage, they combined into their performance some of the stylistic features of Hanju opera, and the musical features of Kunqu opera, Yiyang opera, and Qin opera. It was through this integration that there evolved in Beijing a new form of opera, known as the Peking opera, which has had a history of more than 200 years.

70

京剧不仅要唱，还要表演武术。

Jīngjù bùjǐn yào chàng, hái yào biǎoyǎn wǔshù.

There are not only arias in Peking opera, but performances of martial arts as well.

● 京 剧 不 仅 要 唱， 还 要 表 演
Jīngjù bùjǐn yào chàng, hái yào biǎoyǎn

武 术。
wǔshù.

● 是 啊， 歌 剧 就 没 有 武 术。
Shì a, gējù jiù méiyǒu wǔshù.

● There are not only arias in Peking opera, but performances of martial arts as well.

● Yes, that's true. There is no performance of martial arts in the opera of Western countries.

京剧不仅要唱，还要 _____。
Jīngjù bùjǐn yào chàng, háiyào

说话
shuōhuà

speech

做动作
zuò dòngzuò

action

NOTES

There are two ways to classify roles in Chinese drama: "sheng, dan, jing, mo, chou" and "Sheng, dan, jing, chou". In recent years, in many operas, the role "mo" has been put under the category of "sheng", so people generally classify the roles on the stage of Chinese opera into four basic groups, i.e. "Sheng, dan, jing, chou". Among them "dan" is a general term for female roles, "sheng" and "jing" are terms for male roles, and "chou" is the clown, which is mostly performed by males, except some roles of old women and clown women. "Mo" refers to middle-aged and senior male roles, so they wear beards.

71

怎么有的人是红脸，有的人是白脸呢？
Zěnme yǒude rén shì hóngliǎn, yǒude rén shì báiliǎn ne?

Why do some of the characters have red faces, while others have white faces?

● 怎么有的人是红脸，有的
  Zěnme yǒude rén shì hóngliǎn, yǒude
  人是白脸呢？
  rén shì báiliǎn ne?

● 一般红脸的是好人，白脸
  Yìbān hóngliǎn de shì hǎo rén, báiliǎn
  的是坏人。
  de shì huài rén.

○ Why do some of the characters have red faces, while others have white faces?

● Generally speaking, the character in red is a good guy, while the one in white is a bad guy.

怎么有的人____，有的人____呢？
zěnme yǒude rén　　　　yǒude rén　　　ne

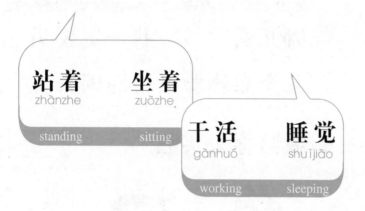

站着 坐着
zhǎnzhe zuòzhe

standing sitting

干活 睡觉
gànhuó shuìjiào

working sleeping

Generally, the facial makeup of the "sheng" and "dan" are much the same. The expression of the uniqueness of the characters is displayed by performance and the costume. Facial painting is applied to the "jing" and "chou". It employs strong and exaggerated colors and fantastic line patterns to change the original faces of the actors. These painted faces make a strong contrast with the light makeup of "sheng" and "dan". Every "jing" and "chou" character has a specific face painting pattern which displays the characteristics of the role, and there are as many face painting patterns as there are "jing" and "chou" characters.

Drama ◎ 戏曲

72

哪儿卖脸谱？
Nǎr   mài   liǎnpǔ?

Where can I buy some face paint?

● **哪儿卖脸谱？我一定要买**
Nǎr   mài liǎnpǔ?   Wǒ yídìng yào mǎi

几个京剧脸谱带回国去。
jǐ gè Jīngjù liǎnpǔ dàihuí guó qù.

● **我陪你去买吧。**
Wǒ péi nǐ qù mǎi ba.

● Where can I buy some face paint? I want to buy some
to take back home.

● Then let me go with you to buy it.

哪儿卖_____?
nǎr　mài

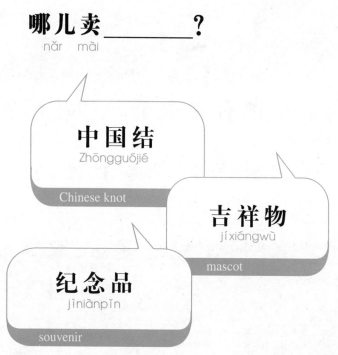

中国结
Zhōngguójié

Chinese knot

吉祥物
jíxiángwù

mascot

纪念品
jìniànpǐn

souvenir

NOTES

　　"Jing" actors, also commonly called "hualian", often perform roles who are robust and gruff in character, such as Guan Yu, Zhang Fei, Cao Cao, Bao Zheng and Lian Po. "Chou" is for the comic clown who is distinguished by the painting on the bridge of the nose and eye sockets. Very often, "chou" actors play amusing roles.

73

中国有多少个戏剧剧种
Zhōngguó yǒu duōshao gè xìjù jùzhǒng?

How many kinds of opera are there in China?

● **中国有多少个戏剧剧种?**
Zhōngguó yǒu duōshao gè xìjù jùzhǒng?

● **大概有300多个呢。**
Dàgài yǒu sānbǎi duō gè ne.

● How many kinds of opera are there in China?
● More than three hundred.

中国有多少个_____?
Zhōngguó yǒu duōshao gè

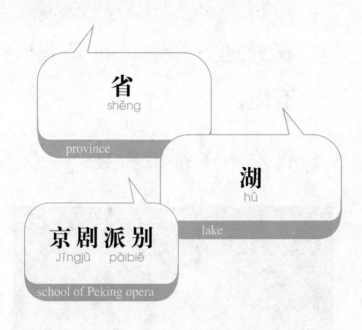

省
shěng

province

湖
hú

lake

京剧派别
Jīngjù   pàibié

school of Peking opera

NOTES

There are approximately more than three hundred kinds of opera in China, among them Peking, Pingju, Yueju, Cantonese, Yuju, and Huangmeixi operas are the most influential.

74

我听过黄梅戏，可是我听不懂。

Wǒ tīngguo Huángméixì, kěshì wǒ tīng bù dǒng.

I've once listened to Huangmeixi, but I couldn't understand it.

● **我听过黄梅戏，可是我听**
Wǒ tīngguo Huángméixì, kěshì wǒ tīng

不懂。
bù dǒng.

● **我差不多都能听懂。**
Wǒ chàbuduō dōu néng tīngdǒng.

● I've once listened to Huangmeixi, but I couldn't understand it.
● I can understand most of it.

我听过_____，可是我听
wǒ tīngguo

不懂。
bū dǒng

kěshì wǒ tīng

京剧
Jīngjù

Peking opera

越剧
Yuèjù

Yueju opera

豫剧
Yūjù

Yuju opera

NOTES

Huangmeixi opera, a kind of local opera in China, was originally known as Huangmeidiao or Caichaxi. Huangmeixi opera originated from the place where Anhui, Hubei and Jiangxi Provinces border on each other. It mainly adopted the tunes of Huangmei Caichadiao, incorporating local folk songs and dances. Later, one troupe went to Anqing in Anhui Province, and the performance began to use the local Anhui dialect, before further evolving into the Huangmeixi opera of today. The traditional repertoire include such plays as *Tianxianpei (A Marriage with a Fairy)* and *Nüfuma (A Female Son-in-Law of the Emperor)*.

Drama ◎ 戏曲

75

"低头思故乡"是哪首诗里的句子?

"Dī tóu sī gùxiāng" shì nǎ shǒu shī li de jùzi?

From which poem does the line "hopelessly homesick as I bowed my head" come?

● "低头思故乡"是哪首诗里

"Dī tóu sī gùxiāng" shì nǎ shǒu shī li

的句子?

de jùzi?

● 是唐诗《静夜思》里的句子。

Shì tángshī Jìngyè Sī li de jùzi.

○ From which poem does the line "hopelessly homesick as I bowed my head" come?

● It's from a Tang poem entitled "Night Thoughts".

"＿＿＿＿＿"是哪首诗里的句子？

shì nǎ shǒu shī li de jūzi

红掌拨清波

hóng zhǎng bō qīng bō

Red palms ply the waves as it oars.

粒粒皆辛苦

lì lì jiē xīnkǔ

Each grain produced through hard toil.

更上一层楼

gèng shàng yì céng lóu

By climbing to a greater height.

NOTES

Tang poems are those written by poets in the Tang Dynasty. "*Night Thoughts*" expresses a nostalgic feeling one has in a quiet night. For thousands of years, the poem has been known by people from all walks of life, even little kids and elderly women. The whole poem reads like this:

The moon shines so brightly besides my bed.

As ground frost I mistook its reflection.

To the moon I lifted my eyes ahead.

Hopelessly homesick as I bowed my head.

76

《静夜思》是谁写的?
Jìngyè Sī   shì shuí xiě de?

Who wrote the poem "*Night Thoughts*"?

● 《静夜思》是谁写的?
　Jìngyè Sī   shì shuí xiě de?

● 是唐朝著名诗人李白写的。
　Shì Tángcháo zhùmíng shīrén Lǐ Bái xiě de.

○ Who wrote the poem "*Night Thoughts*"?

● It was written by the famous Tang Dynasty poet Li Bai.

_____是谁写的?

shì shuí xiě de

《咏鹅》
Yǒng É

Goose

《悯农》
Mǐn Nóng

Toiling Farmers

《登鹳雀楼》
Dēng Guànquèlóu

On the Stork Tower

NOTES

The Tang Dynasty was the golden period for the development of Chinese art and literature. Li Bai was certainly the best known poet of the time. He was called the "immortal poet", for he was bold and bohemian in nature and fond of liquor. He filled his poems with romantic images. Today, we can still read more than 900 poems written by him. Other famous poets of the Tang Dynasty are Du Fu, Li Shangyin, and Bai Juyi.

77

你背过多少首唐诗？

Nǐ   bèiguo   duōshao   shǒu   tángshī?

How many Tang poems have you recited?

● **你背过多少首唐诗？**
Nǐ   bèiguo   duōshao shǒu   tángshī?

● **我曾经背过一些，不过不**
Wǒ céngjīng bèiguo   yìxiē,   búguò bú

太多。
tài duō.

○ How many Tang poems have you recited?

● I once recited some Tang poems, but not many.

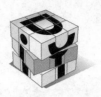

你背过多少首_____?

nǐ bèiguo duōshao shǒu

宋 词

sòngcí

Song poem

元 曲

yuánqǔ

Yuan poem

NOTES

Tang poems that have been handed down amount to about 50,000, which were compiled into the book "*Complete Tang Poetry*" by scholars in the Qing Dynasty. An elementary textbook for learning Tang poems is *Three Hundred Tang Poems*.

78

中国的"四大名著"，你都说得出来吗

Zhōngguó de "sì dà míngzhù", nǐ dōu shuō de chūlái ma?

Can you name the "four great classics" of Chinese literature?

● **中国的"四大名著"，你**
　Zhōngguó de "sì dà míngzhù", nǐ
　都说得出来吗？
　dōu shuō de chūlái ma?

● **它们是《水浒传》、《西**
　Tāmen shì Shuǐhǔ Zhuǎn 、 Xī
　游记》、《三国演义》和
　yóu Jì 、 Sānguó Yǎnyì hé
　《红楼梦》。
　Hónglóu Mèng.

○ Can you name the "four great classics" of Chinese literature?

● They are *Outlaws of the Marsh, Journey to the West, Romance of the Three Kingdoms,* and *Dreams of the Red Mansion.*

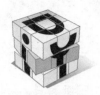

中国的 _____，你都说得
Zhōngguó de   nǐ dōu shuō de

出来吗？
chūlái ma

四大名山
sì dà míngshān

the four well-known mountains

西湖十景
Xīhú   shí jǐng

the ten scenic spots in the West Lake

四个直辖市
sì gè   zhíxiáshì

the four municipalities directly under the Central Government

NOTES

The "four great classics" of ancient Chinese literature refers to four novels written in the Ming and Qing Dynasty. They are *Outlaws of the Marsh* by Shi Nai'an, *Journey to the West* by Wu Cheng'en, *Romance of the Three Kingdoms* by Luo Guanzhong, and *Dreams of the Red Mansion* by the Qing Dynasty author Cao Xueqin.

79

《西游记》和《绿野仙踪》哪个更好看？
Xīyóu Jì hé Lǜyě Xiānzōng nǎge gèng hǎokàn?

Which is better, Journey to the West or The Wonderful Wizard of Oz?

● 《西游记》和《绿野仙踪》
Xīyóu Jì hé Lǜyě Xiānzōng

哪个更好看？
nǎge gèng hǎokàn?

● 都特别好看。
Dōu tèbié hǎokàn.

○ Which is better, *Journey to the West* or *The Wonderful Wizard of Oz*?

● Both are extremely good.

_____ 和 _____ 哪个更好看？
　　　hé　　　nǎge gèng hǎokàn

《水浒传》　《悲惨世界》
Shuǐhǔ Zhuàn　Bēicǎn　Shìjiè

Outlaws of the Marsh　*Las Miserables*

《红楼梦》　《源氏物语》
Hónglóu Mèng　Yuánshì　Wùyǔ

Dreams of the Red Mansion　*The Tales of Genji*

Journey to the West is a mythological novel. It tells the story of Tang Sanzang and his disciples Monkey King, Zhu Bajie and Sha Seng on their way to the Western Paradise. Together they are put through numerous trials and turbulences, finally defeating the demons and monsters. It is based on the true story of a famous Chinese monk, Xuan Zang who went to India to seek the Sutra, the Buddhist holy books. *The Wonderful Wizard of Oz* by American writer Lyman Frank Baum is a classical fairytale, depicting the adventurous journey of a girl named Dorothy with Scarecrow, Lion and Tinman.

80

你觉得什么地方的民歌最好听?
nǐ juéde shénme dìfang de míngē zuì hǎotīng?

Where do you think the best folk songs come from?

● **你觉得什么地方的民歌最好听?**
Nǐ juéde shénme dìfang de míngē zuì hǎotīng?

● **我认为陕北的信天游最好听。**
Wǒ rènwéi Shǎnběi de Xìntiānyóu zuì hǎotīng.

● Where do you think the best folk songs come from?
● I think "Xintianyou" from northern Shaanxi is the best.

你 觉 得 什么 地 方 的
nǐ juéde shénme dìfang de

_____最_____?
　　　　zuì

名胜古迹　　多
míngshèng gǔjì　　duō

historic relics and　　many
scenic spots

气温　　高
qìwēn　　gāo

temperature　　high

NOTES

"Xintianyou", also termed as "shanqu" or "pashandiao", is a popular folk music in northern Shaanxi, Gansu, Ningxia and Inner Mongolia. In the mountainous areas there, working people sing freely using their own words. "Xintianyou" embodies over forty tunes. Themes mainly focus on the love of the young with succinct and vivid words, expressing the rustic feelings of the people.

Literature ◎ 文学

161

81

给我讲一个刘三姐的故事吧。
Gěi wǒ jiǎng yí gè Liú Sānjiě de gùshi ba.

Tell me a story about Liu Sanjie.

● 给我讲一个刘三姐的故事吧。
Gěi wǒ jiǎng yí gè Liú Sānjiě de gùshi ba.

● 好啊，我刚看了一些关于
Hǎo a, wǒ gāng kàn le yìxiē guānyú

她的故事。
tā de gùshi.

○ Tell me a story about Liu Sanjie.

● O.K. I've just read some stories about her.

给我讲一个＿＿＿＿＿＿的
gěi wǒ jiǎng yí gè   de
故事吧。
gùshi ba

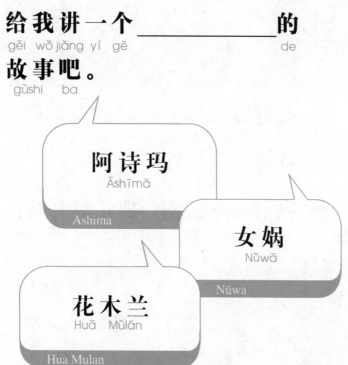

阿诗玛
Āshīmǎ

Ashima

女娲
Nǚwā

Nüwa

花木兰
Huā Mǔlán

Hua Mulan

There are a lot of folklores about Liu Sanjie. These folklores are very popular in places such as Yishan and Liuzhou in Guangxi Province. Liu Sanjie was believed to be an outstanding singer. She was given the title "the Immortal Singer" (Fairy Singer) by the Zhuangs, a minority ethnic group in Guangxi Province, for her love songs and songs that pay tributes to work.

82

我打算暑假去云南旅游。

Wǒ dǎsuàn shǔjià qù Yúnnán lǚyóu.

I'm planning a trip to Yunnan during my summer vacation.

● 我打算暑假去云南旅游，你
Wǒ dǎsuàn shǔjià qù Yúnnán lǚyóu, nǐ

觉得怎么样？
juéde zěnmeyàng?

● 我很喜欢云南，那儿很有特色。
Wǒ hěn xǐhuan Yúnnán, nàr hěn yǒu tèsè.

● I'm planning a trip to Yunnan during my summer vacation.
What do you think of the idea?

● I love Yunnan. You'll find many things with distinctive
local features there.

我打算＿＿＿＿＿＿＿＿。
wǒ dǎsuàn

下个星期回国
xià gè ·xīngqī huí guó

go back home next week

买这种砚台
mǎi zhè zhǒng yàntai

buy an inkslab like this

坐火车去西藏
zuò huǒchē qù Xīzàng

go to Tibet by train

There are altogether 56 nationalities in the People's Republic of China. Apart from the Han nationality, the other 55 nationalities are customarily called minorities because they are small in population. The minorities are widely distributed in provinces and autonomous regions such as Inner Mongolia, Xinjiang, Ningxia, Guangxi, Tibet, Yunnan, Guizhou, Qinghai, Sichuan, Gansu, Liaoning, Jilin, Hunan, Hubei, Hainan and Taiwan. Yunnan has the highest number of nationalities in China, amounting to 25.

83

你去过几次云南？
Nǐ qùguo jǐ cì Yúnnán?

How many times have you been to Yunnan?

- **你去过几次云南？**
  Nǐ qùguo jǐ cì Yúnnán?

- **我去年五月去过一次。**
  Wǒ qùnián wǔ yuè qùguo yí cì.

- How many times have you been to Yunnan?
- I went there once last May.

你去过几次_____？
nǐ qùguo jǐ cì

广西
Guǎngxī

Guangxi

海南
Hǎinán

Hainan

黑龙江
Hēilóngjiāng

Heilongjiang

The population of minorities takes up one-third of the total population of Yunnan Province. Yunnan is famous for the beautiful scenery with different ethnic minority communities scattered in every part of the province. Some of the minorities have their own written languages. For instance the Dais, Tibetans, Yis and Naxis all have their own written languages.

84

你认得出来她是哪个民族的吗？
Nǐ rèn de chūlái tā shì nǎge mínzú de ma?

Can you tell which nationality she comes from?

● 你认得出来她是哪个民族
Nǐ rèn de chūlái tā shì nǎge mínzú

的吗？
de ma?

● 她是位壮族姑娘。
Tā shì wèi Zhuǎngzú gūniang.

● Can you tell which nationality she comes from?
● She is a girl from the Zhuang nationality.

你认得出来她是哪个 ____ 的吗？
nǐ rèn de chūlái tā shì nǎge ____ de ma

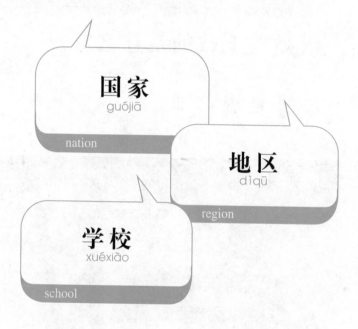

国家
guójiā

nation

地区
dìqū

region

学校
xuéxiào

school

Zhuang is the minority ethnic group that has the largest number of population in China. Its people live mainly in Guangxi Autonomous Region. Languages of five nationalities are printed on Chinese Renminbi. Besides Chinese, there are also Mongolian, Tibetan, Uygur and Zhuang languages.

169

85

她头上戴的是什么?

Tā tóu shang dài de shì shénme?

What does she wear on her head?

● **她头上戴的是什么?**
Tā tóu shang dài de shì shénme?

● **那是银首饰。**
Nà shì yín shǒushi.

○ What does she wear on her head?
○ Those are silver ornaments.

她____上戴的是什么？
tā shang dài de shì shénme

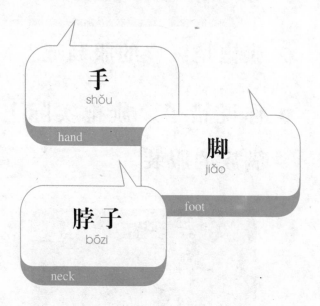

手
shǒu
hand

脚
jiǎo
foot

脖子
bōzi
neck

Nationalities ◎ 民族

86

旗袍是汉族的服装吧？

Qípáo shì Hànzú de fúzhuāng ba?

The Qipao is the costume of the Han nationality, isn't it?

○ **旗袍是汉族的服装吧？**
Qípáo shì Hànzú de fúzhuāng ba?

● **你说错了，旗袍实际上是满族的服装。**
Nǐ shuō cuò le, qípáo shíjì shang shì Mǎnzú de fúzhuāng.

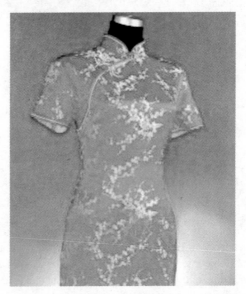

○ The Qipao is the costume of the Han nationality, isn't it?
● You are wrong. Actually Qipao was derived from the Manchu dress.

旗袍是_____的服装吧？
qípáo shì de fúzhuāng ba

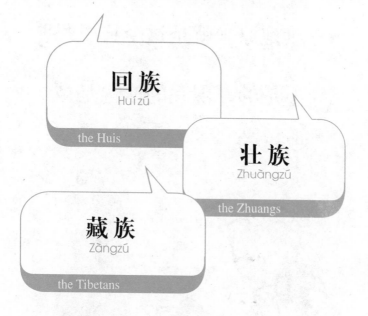

回族
Huízú

the Huis

壮族
Zhuǎngzú

the Zhuangs

藏族
Zàngzú

the Tibetans

NOTES

The Manchus mainly live in the Northeastern Provinces of China — Liaoning, Jinlin, and Heilongjiang, among which Liaoning has the largest population. The Qing Dynasty that ruled the country from 1644 to 1911 was established by the Manchus. Altogether 12 emperors reigned during the Qing Dynasty.

87

现在的旗袍是被改过的。

Xiànzài de qípáo shì bèi gǎiguo de.

The qipao today has been altered.

● **旗袍原来就是这个样子吗？**
Qípáo yuánlái jiùshì zhège yàngzi ma?

● **不是的，现在的旗袍是被**
Bú shì de, xiànzài de qípáo shì bèi

改过的。
gǎiguo de.

● Does the qipao today look like it did in the past?
● No, the qipao today has been altered.

现在的_____是被改过的。

xiànzài de　　　　　shì bèi gǎiguo de

唐装
tángzhuāng

tangzhuang

和服
héfú

kimono

牛仔裤
niúzǎikù

blue jeans

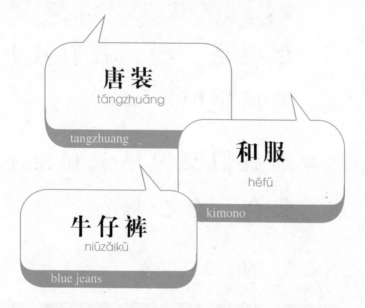

NOTES

The qipao was originally the costume of a minority people, the Manchus. The Manchus have been termed as "qiren", which is why the dress they wear is called qipao. The qipao worn by Manchu women was originally loose in the waist. Later, the design changed to make qipao tight in waist to fit the body of women. The altered qipao has become the traditional costume for Chinese women.

88

你要是有空，我们就去放风筝吧？
Nǐ yàoshì yǒu kōng, wǒmen jiù qù fàng fēngzheng ba?

Let's go and fly a kite if you can spare the time!

● 你要是有空，我们就去
Nǐ yàoshì yǒu kōng, wǒmen jiù qù

放风筝吧？
fàng fēngzheng ba?

● 那我们明天早上在楼下
Nà wǒmen míngtiān zǎoshang zài lóu xià

集合，怎么样？
jíhé, zěnmeyàng?

● 好的。
Hǎode.

● Let's go and fly a kite if you can spare the time!
● Then how about we meet outside the building tomorrow morning?
● Yes, that's a deal.

你要是 _____，我们 就
nǐ yàoshì wǒmen jiù

去 放 风筝 吧？
qù fàng fēngzheng ba

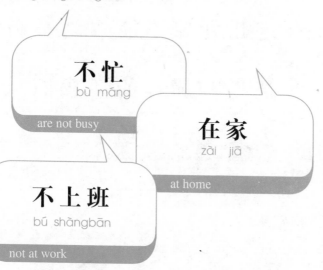

不 忙
bù máng

are not busy

在家
zài jiā

at home

不 上班
bù shàngbān

not at work

NOTES

The invention of kites may date back to the Warring States Period in Chinese history. It was said that a deft carpenter Lu Ban invented wooden kites. In the Han Dynasty, due to the invention and application of paper, people began to make paper kites instead of the wooden kites, naming this new kind of kite "paper glede" or "zhǐyuān". During the Five Dynasties, people tied bamboo whistles on the kites, which were blown by the wind. The sound the whistle made was very much like the sound of a zither, so this kind of kite was named "fēngzheng" (wind zither).

Customs ◎ 民俗

89

这儿好像不能放风筝啊!
Zhèr hǎoxiàng bū néng fàng fēngzheng a!

We cannot possibly fly the kite here!

● 这儿好像不能放风筝啊!
Zhèr hǎoxiàng bū néng fàng fēngzheng a!

● 是吗? 那样的话我们只好
Shì ma? Nàyàng de huà wǒmen zhǐhǎo

去天安门广场了。
qù Tiān'ānmén Guǎngchǎng le.

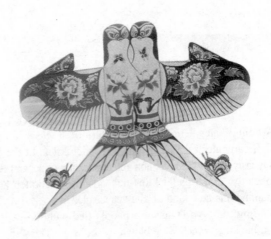

● We cannot possibly fly the kite here!

● Oh? Then we have to go to Tian'anmen Square to fly it.

这儿好像不能_____啊。

zhèr hǎoxiàng bù néng a

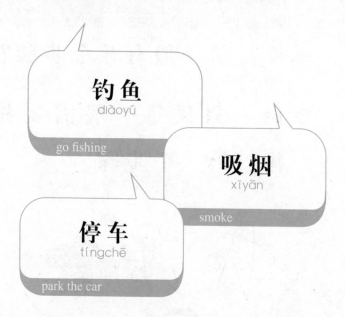

钓鱼
diàoyú

go fishing

吸烟
xīyān

smoke

停车
tíngchē

park the car

NOTES

The first kite was designed for military purpose. Ancient people used kites for military detection and transfer. Since the Tang Dynasty, kites gradually became a tool for entertainment in people's daily life. In China, spring is the high time to fly kites.

90

做风筝一般有几个步骤？
Zuò fēngzheng yìbān yǒu jǐ gè bùzhòu?

How many steps does it take to make a kite?

● 做风筝一般有几个步骤？
Zuò fēngzheng yìbān yǒu jǐ gè bùzhòu?

● 做一只风筝一般需要扎、
Zuò yì zhī fēngzheng yìbān xūyào zhā,

糊、绘三个步骤。
hū, huì sān gè bùzhòu.

○ How many steps does it take to make a kite?

● Generally speaking, there are three steps to make a kite:
binding, pasting and painting.

_____一般有几个步骤？
yìbān yǒu jǐ gè bùzhōu

办护照
bàn hùzhào
apply for a passport

品茶
pǐn chá
savor tea

做月饼
zuò yuèbǐng
make a moon cake

NOTES

The first step to make a kite is to do the "binding", that is to say, to make the framework of the kite with fine bamboo stripes. The second step is "pasting", which means to paste materials such as paper or silk onto the framework of the kite. "Painting" involves drawing various patterns on the kite with colorful pigments. After finishing the above steps, one can go and fly the kite. "Binding", "pasting", "painting" and "flying" are the "Four Skills of Kites".

Customs ◎ 民俗

91

把这对窗花送给我，好不好？
Bǎ zhè duì chuānghuā sòng gěi wǒ, hǎobuhǎo?

Could you give me this pair of paper-cuts?

● 把这对窗花送给我，好不好？
Bǎ zhè duì chuānghuā sòng gěi wǒ, hǎobuhǎo?

● 好啊。
Hǎo a.

○ Could you give me this pair of paper-cuts?

● Certainly.

把＿＿＿＿＿＿送给我，好不好？
bǎ　　　　　　　sòng gěi wǒ　　hǎobuhǎo

这个礼物
zhège　lǐwù

this present

这束花
zhè shù huā

the bunch of flowers

那本字典
nà běn　zìdiǎn

that dictionary

NOTES

　　　　Paper-cutting is one of the most popular folk arts in China. Its history can be traced back to the 6th century. Paper-cuts for window decoration are the main variety. In days of celebration, for instance during the Dragon Boat Festival, Spring Festival or at a wedding ceremony, people decorate doors and windows with paper-cuts. People find hope and comfort in expressing wishes with paper-cuts.

Customs ◎ 民俗

92

你剪的是什么图案？

Nǐ jiǎn de shì shénme tú'àn?

What pattern did you cut?

● **你剪的是什么图案？**

Nǐ jiǎn de shì shénme tú'àn?

● **我为你剪了一幅"喜鹊登梅"。**

Wǒ wèi nǐ jiǎn le yì fú "xǐ què dēngméi"

○ What pattern did you cut?
● I cut a picture called "xique dengmei"
(pied magpies on a plum branch).

你____的是什么____？
nǐ ____ de shì shénme ____

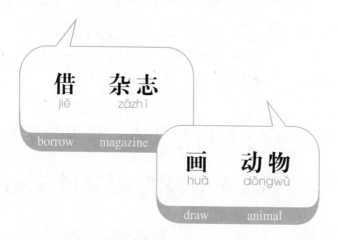

借　杂志
jiè　zázhì

borrow　magazine

画　动物
huà　dòngwù

draw　animal

Chinese paper-cutting has numerous patterns. Chinese characters, birds and beasts, human figures, plants and flowers, immortals, painted masks, and scenes of daily life all constitute the patterns of paper-cutting. "Xique dengmei" (pied magpies on a plum branch) is a popular pattern in the villages of Shanxi Province and gives a genuine expression of local country life.

Customs ◉ 民俗

93

除了杨柳青以外，还有哪儿有年画儿？

Chúle Yángliǔqīng yǐwài, hǎiyǒu nǎr yǒu niánhuàr?

Apart from Yangliuqing, where are Nianhua (New Year woodblock prints) available?

● 除了杨柳青以外，还有哪儿有

Chúle Yángliǔqīng yǐwài, hǎiyǒu nǎr yǒu

年画儿？

niánhuàr?

● 除了杨柳青以外，苏州的桃花坞

Chúle Yángliǔqīng yǐwài, Sūzhōu de Táohuāwù

和潍坊的杨家埠也都制作年画儿。

hé Wéifāng de Yángjiābù yě dōu zhìzuò niánhuàr.

● Apart from Yangliuqing, where are Nianhua (New Year woodblock prints) available?

● Apart from Yangliuqing, Taohuawu in Suzhou and Yangjiabu in Weifang make Nianhua (New Year woodblock prints) as well.

除了＿＿＿＿以外，还有哪儿有
chúle　　　　　　yǐwài　　hǎiyǒu　nǎr　yǒu

＿＿＿＿？

苏州　　**丝绸**
Sūzhōu　　sīchóu

Suzhou　　silk

哈尔滨　　**冰灯**
Hā'ěrbīn　　bīngdēng

Ha'erbin　　ice lantern

北京　　**烤鸭**
Běijīng　　kǎoyā

Beijing　　roast duck

NOTES

The origin of Nianhua (New Year woodblock prints) can be traced back to the peach talisman people pasted on their gates in ancient times. Nianhua prints thrived in the Ming and Qing Dynasties. Many Nianhua printing centers were established at that time, including Taohuawu in Suzhou, Yangliuqing in Tianjin, Yangjiabu in Shandong Province, Mianzhu in Sichuan Province, Wuqiang in Hebei Province, Foshan in Guangdong Province and Zhuxianzhen in Henan Province.

Customs ◎ 民俗

94

这附近有卖年画儿的吗？
Zhè fùjìn yǒu mài niánhuàr de ma?

Can I buy Nianhua somewhere nearby?

● 这附近有卖年画儿的吗？
Zhè fùjìn yǒu mài niánhuàr de ma?

● 前边就有一家。
Qiánbian jiù yǒu yì jiā.

● Can I buy Nianhua somewhere nearby?

● There is a shop selling Nianhua over there.

这附近有_____吗?
zhè fùjìn yǒu _____ ma

菜市场
càishìchǎng

food market

饭店
fàndiàn

restaurant

修车的
xiū chē de

garage

Traditional Nianhua prints reflect the customs of the local people. Auspicious images such as a fish and a boy, trinity of star gods symbolizing good fortune, official salary, longevity, a stout boy, and a bumper harvest are among the most popular.

95

你们这次去少林寺玩儿得怎么样?
Nǐmen zhè cì qù Shàolínsì wánr de zěnmeyàng?

How was your trip to Shaolin Temple?

● 你们这次去少林寺玩儿得
Nǐmen zhè cì qù Shàolínsì wánr de

怎么样?
zěnmeyàng?

● 我们又看风景又学功夫,
Wǒmen yòu kàn fēngjǐng yòu xué gōngfu,

可高兴了!
kě gāoxìng le!

● How was your trip to Shaolin Temple?
● Exciting! We enjoyed the scenery as well learned some martial arts (gongfu).

你们这次去＿＿玩儿得怎么样？

nǐmen zhè cì qù ＿＿ wánr de zěnmeyàng

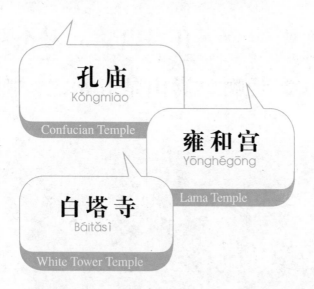

孔庙
Kǒngmiào

Confucian Temple

雍和宫
Yōnghégōng

Lama Temple

白塔寺
Báitǎsì

White Tower Temple

Shaolin Temple is located in the Song Mountain region, at the foot of Shaoshi Mountain, 15-kilometer northwest of Dengfeng City, Henan Province. Thick forests surround the temple, giving it a quiet atmosphere. Shaolin Temple got its name from this remote and quiet environment, which means "the temple hidden in the thick forests of Shaoshi Mountain".

Geography ◎ 地理

96

少林寺在嵩山上，对不对？
Shǎolínsì zài Sōngshān shang, duìbuduì?

Shaolin Temple is on Song Mountain, isn't it?

● 少林寺在嵩山上，对不对？
Shǎolínsì zài Sōngshān shang, duìbuduì?

● 是啊，嵩山是五岳之一呢。
Shì a, Sōngshān shì wǔyuè zhī yī ne.

○ Shaolin Temple is on Song Mountain, isn't it?

● Yes, it is. Song Mountain is among the "Five Sacred Mountains".

_____ 在 _____ , 对不对 ？
zài　　　　　duìbuduì

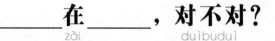

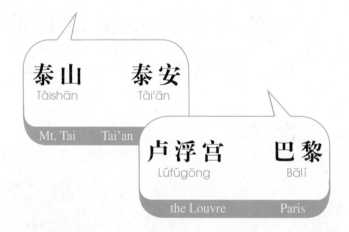

泰山　　　泰安
Tàishān　　Tài'ān

Mt. Tai　　Tai'an

卢浮宫　　巴黎
Lúfúgōng　　Bālí

the Louvre　　　Paris

NOTES

There are five well-known mountains in China, which are termed "the Five Sacred Mountains". The Song Mountain in Dengfeng City, Henan Province is the Central Mountain among the five. The other four mountains are the East Mountain— Tai Mountain in Tai'an, Shangdong Province, the West Mountain—Hua Mountain in Huayin, Shaanxi Province, the South Mountain—Heng Mountain in Hengshan, Hunan Province and the North Mountain—Heng Mountain in Hunyuan, Shanxi Province.

Geography ◎ 地理

97

听说长江是中国最长的河。

Tīngshuō Chángjiāng shì Zhōngguó zuì cháng de hé,

I hear that the Yangtze River is the longest river in China.

● 听说长江是中国最长的
Tīngshuō Chángjiāng shì Zhōngguó zuì cháng de

河，对吗？

hé, duì·ma?

● 没错。

Méicuò.

● I hear that the Yangtze River is the longest river in China, isn't it?

● Yes, you are right.

听说＿＿＿是中国最长的河，
tīngshuō　　　　shì Zhōngguó zuì cháng de hé

对吗？
duì ma

黄河
Huánghé

the Yellow River

辽河
Liáohé

the Liao River

淮河
Huáihé

the Huai River

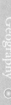

NOTES

　　The Yangtze River is over 6,300 kilometers in length with great water flow and is the third longest river in the world. The name Yangtze was originally used to refer to the lower reaches of the river. However, because this was the first name heard by missionaries, it has been applied in English to the entire river.

98

长江长是长，不过中国人的母亲河是黄河。

Chángjiāng chángshicháng, búguò Zhōngguórén de mǔqīnhé shì Huánghé.

The Yangtze River is long indeed, but the mother river of the Chinese is the Yellow River.

● 长江长是长，不过中国人

Chángjiāng chángshicháng, búguò Zhōngguórén

的母亲河是黄河。

de mǔqīnhé shì Huánghé.

● 你知道的还真不少！

Nǐ zhīdào de hái zhēn bù shǎo!

● The Yangtze River is long indeed, but the mother river of the Chinese is the Yellow River.

● You know so much about China.

_____是_____，不过我不喜欢。
shì　　　　　búguò wǒ bù xǐhuan

漂亮
piàoliang

pretty

便宜
piányi

cheap

好
hǎo

good

The Yellow River, with a total length of 5,464 kilometers, is the second longest river in China, second to the Yangtze River. The Yellow River is the birthplace of ancient Chinese culture and the cradle of Chinese Civilization. The Yellow River region was, for a considerably long period of time, the center of politics, economics and culture in China, so it was entitled "the Mother River" by the Chinese people.

Geography ◎ 地理

99

山西和陕西哪个大？
Shānxī hé Shǎnxī nǎge dà?

Which is larger, Shanxi or Shaanxi?

● 山西和陕西哪个大？
　Shānxī hé Shǎnxī nǎge dà?

● 山西没有陕西大。
　Shānxī méiyǒu Shǎnxī dà.

陕西省　延安　西安　大同　太原　山西省

● Which is larger, Shanxi or Shaanxi?
● Shanxi is smaller in size.

山西和陕西哪个_____？
Shānxī hé Shǎnxī nǎge

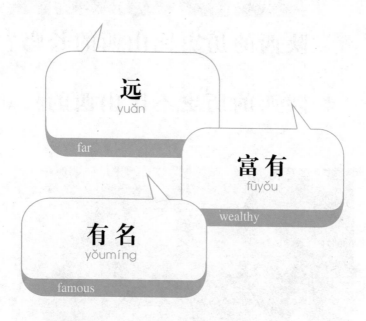

远
yuǎn

far

富有
fùyǒu

wealthy

有名
yǒumíng

famous

China is divided into 34 province level administrative units, which include 23 provinces, 5 autonomous regions, 4 municipalities directly under the Central Government and 2 special administrative regions. The Xinjiang Uygur Autonomous Region is the largest province level administrative unit.

Geography ◎ 地理

100

陕西的历史不比山西的长。
Shǎnxī de lìshǐ bù bǐ Shānxī de cháng.

The history of Shaanxi is no longer than that of Shanxi.

● 陕西的历史比山西的长吗？
Shǎnxī de lìshǐ bǐ Shānxī de cháng ma?

● 陕西的历史不比山西的长。
Shǎnxī de lìshǐ bù bǐ Shānxī de cháng.

○ Does Shaanxi have a longer history than Shanxi?
● The history of Shaanxi is no longer than that of Shanxi.

陕西的历史不比山西的_____。
Shǎnxī de lìshǐ bù bǐ Shānxī de

短
duǎn

short

悠久
yōujiǔ

long

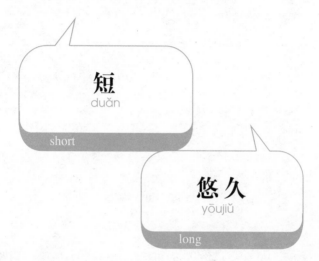

Shaanxi Province boasts a long history, with numerous spots of historic interest, such as the terracotta warriors and horses, the Big Goose Pagoda and the Forest of Stone Steles Museum. The provincial capital city Xi'an (previously named Chang'an) is termed as "the thousand-year capital" of China. Shanxi is named after its location in the west of the Taihang Mountain Range. It also has a very long history. The provincial capital is Taiyuan. Shanxi is well-known for the rich coal resources, which have earned it the title "the sea of coal".

十二属相
12 Chinese Years of Animals

The names of 12 symbolic animals are associated with a 12-year cycle. Every animal is used to denote the year of a person's birth.

鼠(shǔ) rat
1948, 1960, 1972,
1984, 1996, 2008

牛(niú) ox
1949, 1961, 1973,
1985, 1997, 2009

虎(hǔ) tiger
1950, 1962, 1974,
1986, 1998, 2010

兔(tù) rabbit
1951, 1963, 1975,
1987, 1999, 2011

龙(lóng) dragon
1952, 1964, 1976,
1988, 2000, 2012

蛇(shé) snake
1953, 1965, 1977,
1989, 2001, 2013

马(mǎ) horse
1954, 1966, 1978,
1990, 2002, 2014

猴(hóu) monkey
1956, 1968, 1980,
1992, 2004, 2016

羊(yáng) sheep
1955, 1967, 1979,
1991, 2003, 2015

鸡(jī) rooster
1957, 1969, 1981,
1993, 2005, 2017

狗(gǒu) dog
1958, 1970, 1982,
1994, 2006, 2018

猪(zhū) pig
1959, 1971, 1983,
1995, 2007, 2019

中国的节日
Zhōngguó de jiérì
Chinese Holidays

元旦 Yuándàn	New Year's Day (January 1st)
春节 Chūnjié	Spring Festival (the 1st day of the 1st lunar month)
元宵节 Yuánxiāojié	Lantern Festival (the 15th day of the 1st lunar month)
妇女节 Fùnǚjié	International Women's Day (March 8th)
植树节 Zhíshùjié	Arbor Day (March 12th)
国际消费者 Guójì Xiāofèizhě 权益日 Quányìrì	World Consumer Right Day (March 15th)
清明节 Qīngmíngjié	Tomb-sweeping Day (April 5th)
国际劳动节 Guójì Láodòngjié	International Labor Day (May 1st)
青年节 Qīngniánjié	Chinese Youth Day (May 4th)

端午节 Duānwǔjié	Dragon Boat Festival (the 5th day of the 5th lunar month)
国际儿童节 Guójì Értóngjié	International Children's Day (June 1st)
中国共产党 Zhōngguó Gòngchǎndǎng **诞生纪念日** Dànshēn Jìniànrì	Anniversary of the Founding of the Chinese Communist Party (July 1st)
七夕情人节 Qīxī Qíngrénjié	Double Seventh Festival/ Chinese Valentine's Day (the 7th day of the 7th lunar month)
建军节 Jiànjūnjié	Army Day (August 1st)
教师节 Jiàoshījié	Teacher's Day (September 10th)
国庆节 Guóqìngjié	National Day (October 1st)
中秋节 Zhōngqiūjié	Mid-Autumn Festival (the 15th day of the 8th lunar month)
重阳节 Chóngyángjié	Double Ninth Festival (the 9th day of the 9th lunar month)

中国历史年代简表

Zhōngguó lìshǐ niándài jiǎnbiǎo

A Brief Chinese Chronology

五帝 Wǔdì	Five August Emperors (c. 30th century B.C. — c. 21st century B.C.)
夏 Xià	Xia Dynasty (c. 2070 B.C.— 1600 B.C.)
商 Shāng	Shang Dynasty (1600 B.C. — 1046 B.C.)
西周 Xīzhōu	Western Zhou Dynasty (1046 B.C. — 771 B.C.)
东周 Dōngzhōu	Eastern Zhou Dynasty (770 B.C. — 256 B.C.)
秦 Qín	Qin Dynasty (221 B.C. — 206 B.C.)
西汉 Xīhàn	Western Han Dynasty (206 B.C. — A.D. 25)
东汉 Dōnghàn	Eastern Han Dynasty (25—220)
三国 Sānguó	Three Kingdoms (220—280)
西晋 Xījìn	Western Jin Dynasty (265—317)
东晋 Dōngjìn	Eastern Jin Dynasty (317—420)

南北朝 Nánběicháo	Southern and Northern Dynasties (420—589)
隋 Suí	Sui Dynasty (581—618)
唐 Táng	Tang Dynasty (618—907)
五代 Wǔdài	Five Dynasties (907—960)
宋 Sòng	Song Dynasty (960—1279)
元 Yuán	Yuan Dynasty (1206—1368)
明 Míng	Ming Dynasty (1368—1644)
清 Qīng	Qing Dynasty (1616—1911)
中华民国 Zhōnghuá Mínguó	Republic of China（1912—1949）

中华人民共和国1949年10月1日成立
Zhōnghuá Rénmín Gōnghéguó 1949 nián 10 yuè 1 rì Chénglì
Founding of the People's Republic of China on October 1, 1949

郑 重 声 明

　　高等教育出版社依法对本书享有专有出版权。任何未经许可的复制、销售行为均违反《中华人民共和国著作权法》,其行为人将承担相应的民事责任和行政责任,构成犯罪的,将被依法追究刑事责任。为了维护市场秩序,保护读者的合法权益,避免读者误用盗版书造成不良后果,我社将配合行政执法部门和司法机关对违法犯罪的单位和个人给予严厉打击。社会各界人士如发现上述侵权行为,希望及时举报,本社将奖励举报有功人员。

反盗版举报电话:(010) 58581897/58581896/58581879

传　　真:(010) 82086060

E – mail: dd@hep.com.cn

通信地址:北京市西城区德外大街 4 号

　　　　　　高等教育出版社打击盗版办公室

邮　　编:100120

购书请拨打电话:(010)58581118

图书在版编目（CIP）数据

体验汉语 100 句. 文化类：英语版 ／ 孙易, 孙雪, 谷峰
编. —北京：高等教育出版社, 2007.1 (2009 重印)
ISBN 978 – 7 – 04 – 020523 – 7

Ⅰ. 体…　Ⅱ. ①孙…②孙…③谷…　Ⅲ. 汉语 – 口语 – 对
外汉语教学 – 自学参考资料　Ⅳ. H195.4

中国版本图书馆 CIP 数据核字（2007）第 001073 号

出版发行	高等教育出版社	**购书热线**	010 – 58581118
社　　址	北京市西城区德外大街 4 号	**免费咨询**	800 – 810 – 0598
邮政编码	100120	**网　　址**	http://www.hep.edu.cn
总　　机	010 – 58581000		http://www.hep.com.cn
		网上订购	http://www.landraco.com
			http://www.landraco.com.cn
经　　销	蓝色畅想图书发行有限公司	**畅想教育**	http://www.widedu.com
印　　刷	高等教育出版社印刷厂		
开　　本	889 × 1194　1/32		
印　　张	6.75	**版　　次**	2007 年 1 月第 1 版
字　　数	160 000	**印　　次**	2009 年 4 月第 3 次印刷